AF411979

TRANSIENT CONFESSIONS

TRANSIENT CONFESSIONS

Corinne L. Rusch

KERBER PHOTO ART

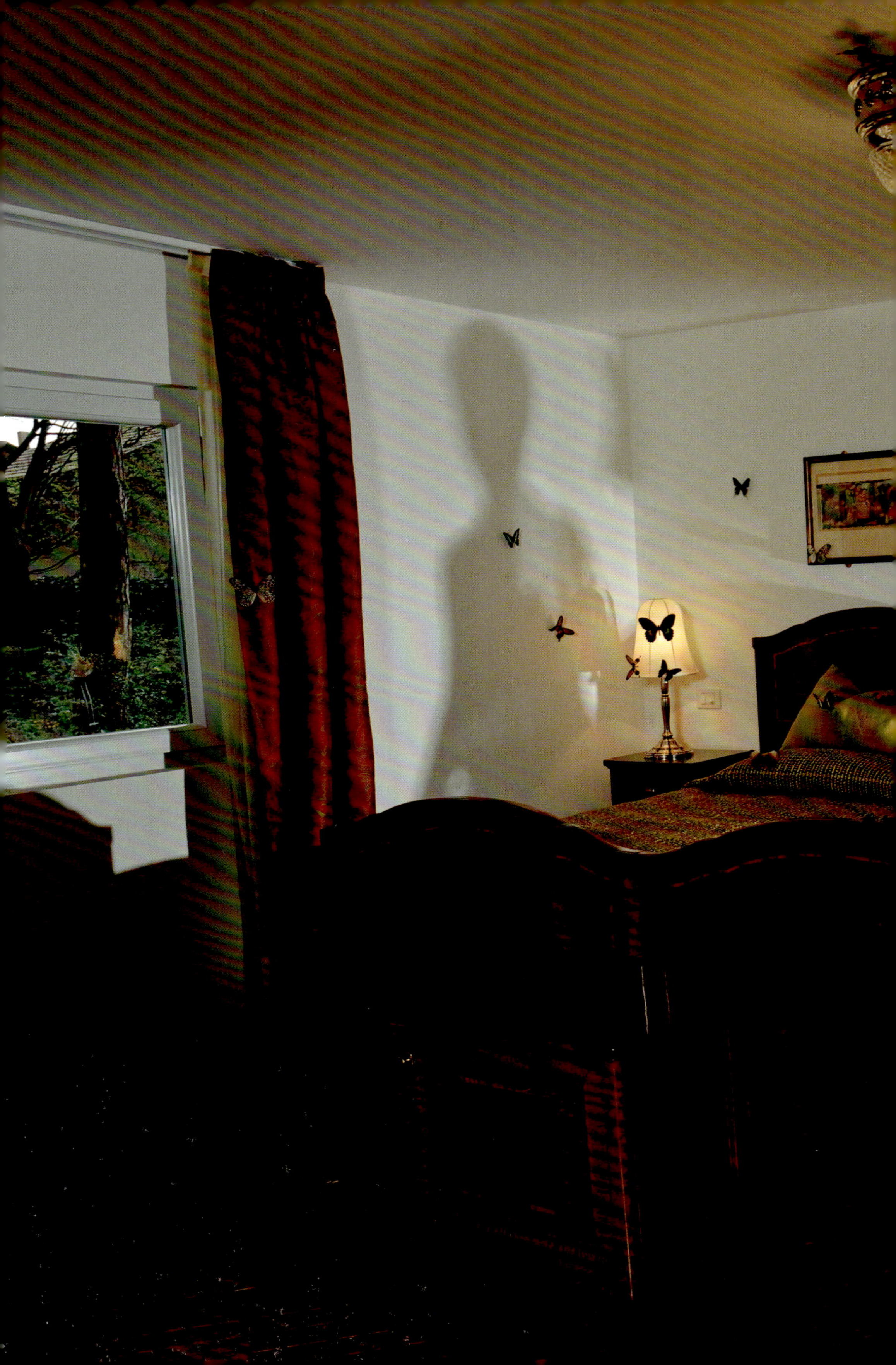

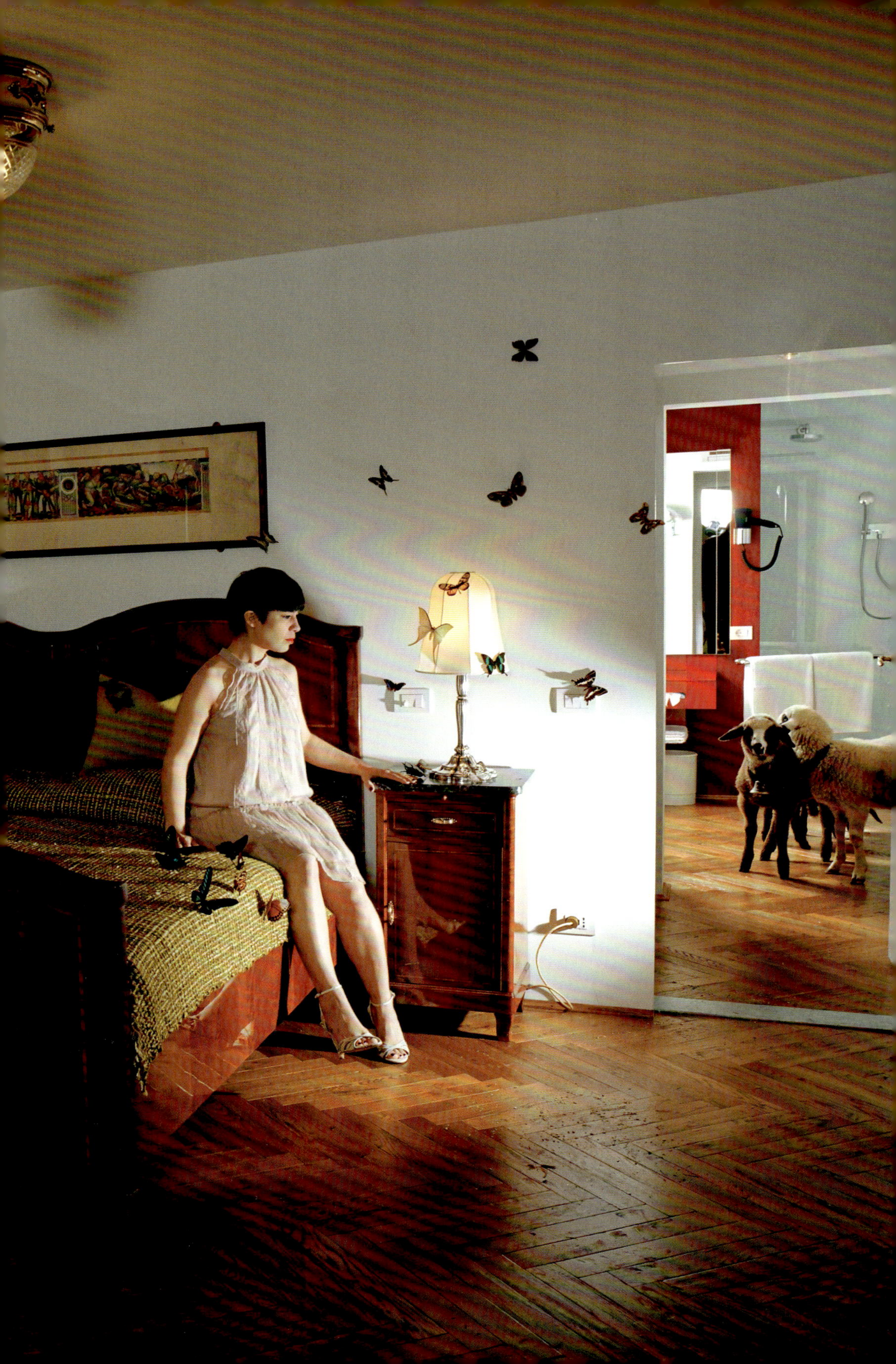

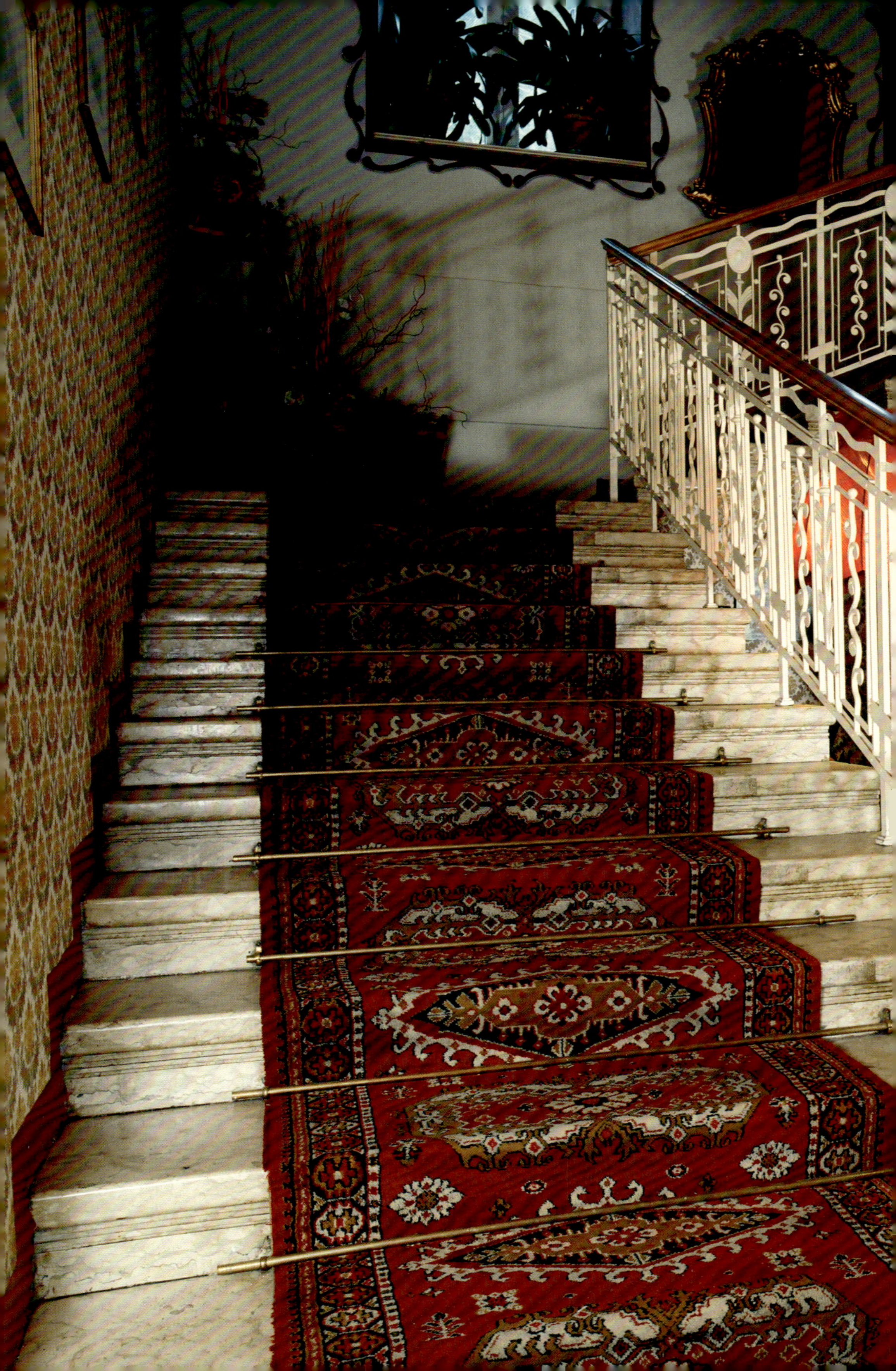

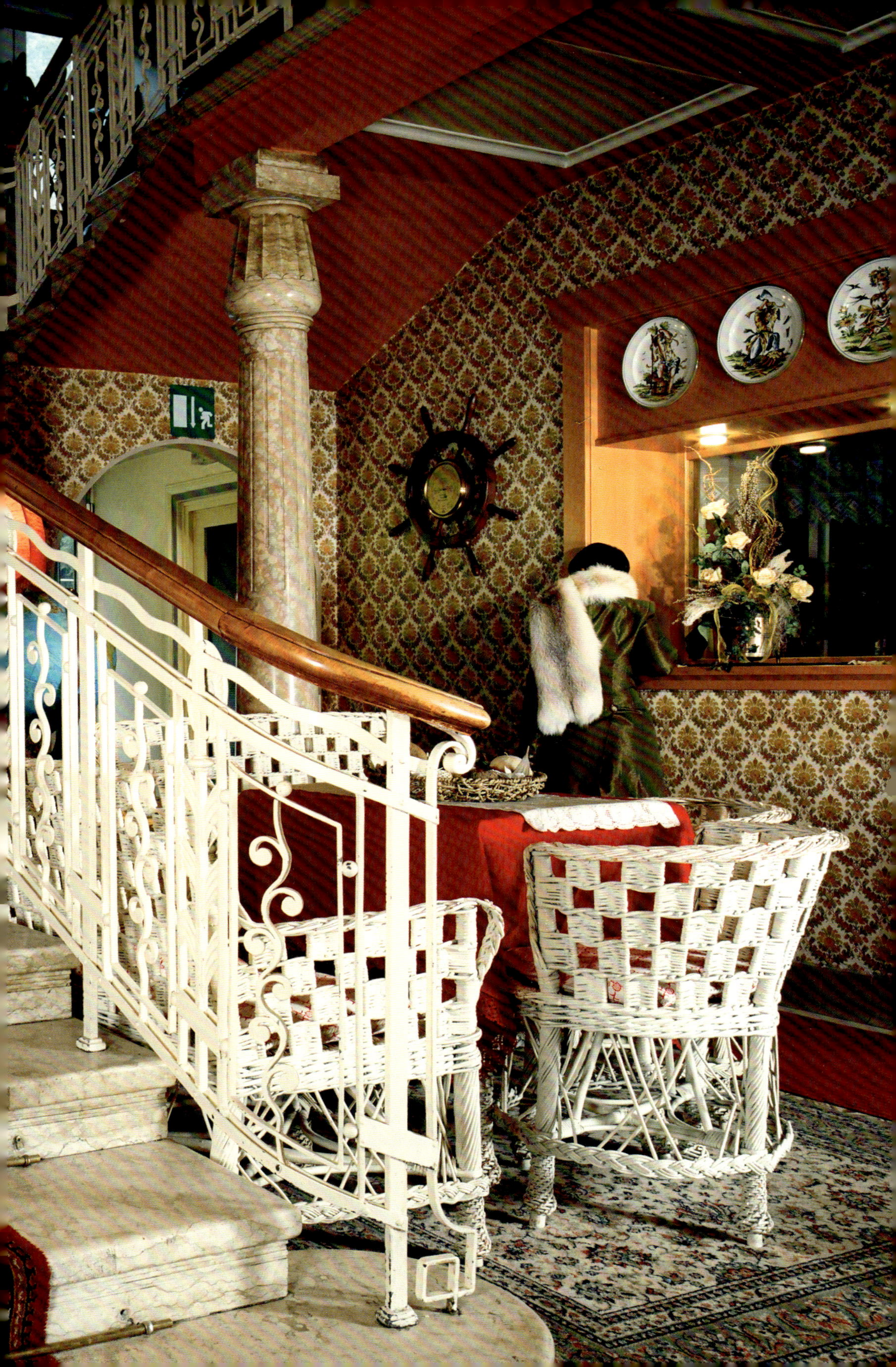

Forward

Fallaces sunt rerum species – Seneca

*

Perhaps it would be more fitting if I ally myself at first with the great poet Catullus, asking, "Cui dono lepidum novum libellum?" Or like Shelley, I could turn with that bouquet of flowers in my outstretched hand, to find?

It is true that as the population swells and overflows its boundaries, there are many places that have lost the benefit of solitude, the once plentiful, small, silent retreats that offer solace from the bustle and press that are the result of human cohabitation. As these places of necessary respite vanish one by one from our landscapes, we may well assume that our connexion to those living around us has, by necessity, improved. Should not proximity be the father of acquaintance? Would it not seem logical to conclude that friendship and camaraderie should be the natural offspring of propinquity?

This, alas, is not the case!

On the contrary, my friends, those among you who are city dwellers may have yourself noticed an increasing sense of isolation, of imposed solitude, as the tide of citizens around you has increased. Indeed, it seems that this brings out the worst in men. If Shelley were to turn today on a crowded street, he might find not a soul willing to accept his lovely offering, so cold and haughty have become the members of the human race who live piled in our cities!

So what are we to make of this puzzling situation? And how may we, in light of progress, attempt to solve it with the best intentions for the future of our fellow man? We may find a certain kind of quaint example for improvement in the small village hostelry or inn, a well proven model of cohabitation that shall provide the basis for my investigation.

This volume is divided into three parts, the first of which delineates the most excellent qualities of composed solitude to be found in the aforementioned village inns, of which I have selected several. They have been chosen on the basis of their varying situation, proportions, and overall character, in an attempt to show that these differences prove little obstacle to the similarities I wish to establish. The second part is a shadow to the first; that is to say, I will outline the sad history of the slow degradation of our cities and large towns and the ramification

KARNER BLUE BUTTERFLY
Lycaeides melissa samuelis, gossamer wing family
Nabokov 1944

Imperiled (NatureServe status G2)

A diminutive specimen with a wingspan less than one inch in size, the male has deep indigo wings with white edges, the female blue wings more muted than those of the male, with orange spots on the hindwings. Their natural habitat is the Northeastern and Central United States, first recorded in the Hudson Valley at Karner, New York. The Karner Blue is recognized as extinct in certain parts of Canada. Endangered status is seen as the result of habitat fragmentation through forest cultivation practices and human habitation, which inhibit normal population growth, as does the culling of wild lupine, *Lupinus perennis*, a favorite butterfly food and the leaves of which are the sole source of nourishment for the insect in the larval stage. The Karner Blue is multivoltine, breeding twice a year, typically in late April and early summer, closely following the phenology of wild lupine. The species depends on a heterogeneous habitat and prefers a mosaic of sun and shade, reflecting the different requirements of their stages of development.

This particular specimen was first recognized as a distinct species by Vladimir Nabokov–well-known author of several novels, including *Lolita* (1955) and *Pale Fire* (1962)–who was curator of lepidoptera at Harvard University's Museum of Comparative Zoology in the 1940s. The Karner Blue was one of the many "Polyommatus blues" in Nabokov's theory surmising that these particular butterflies were of Asian origin, and made their way to the American continent via the Bering Strait in a series of waves. Nabokov describes a group of these tiny butterflies in his novel *Pnin* (1957), depicting them as a mass of "blue snowflakes."

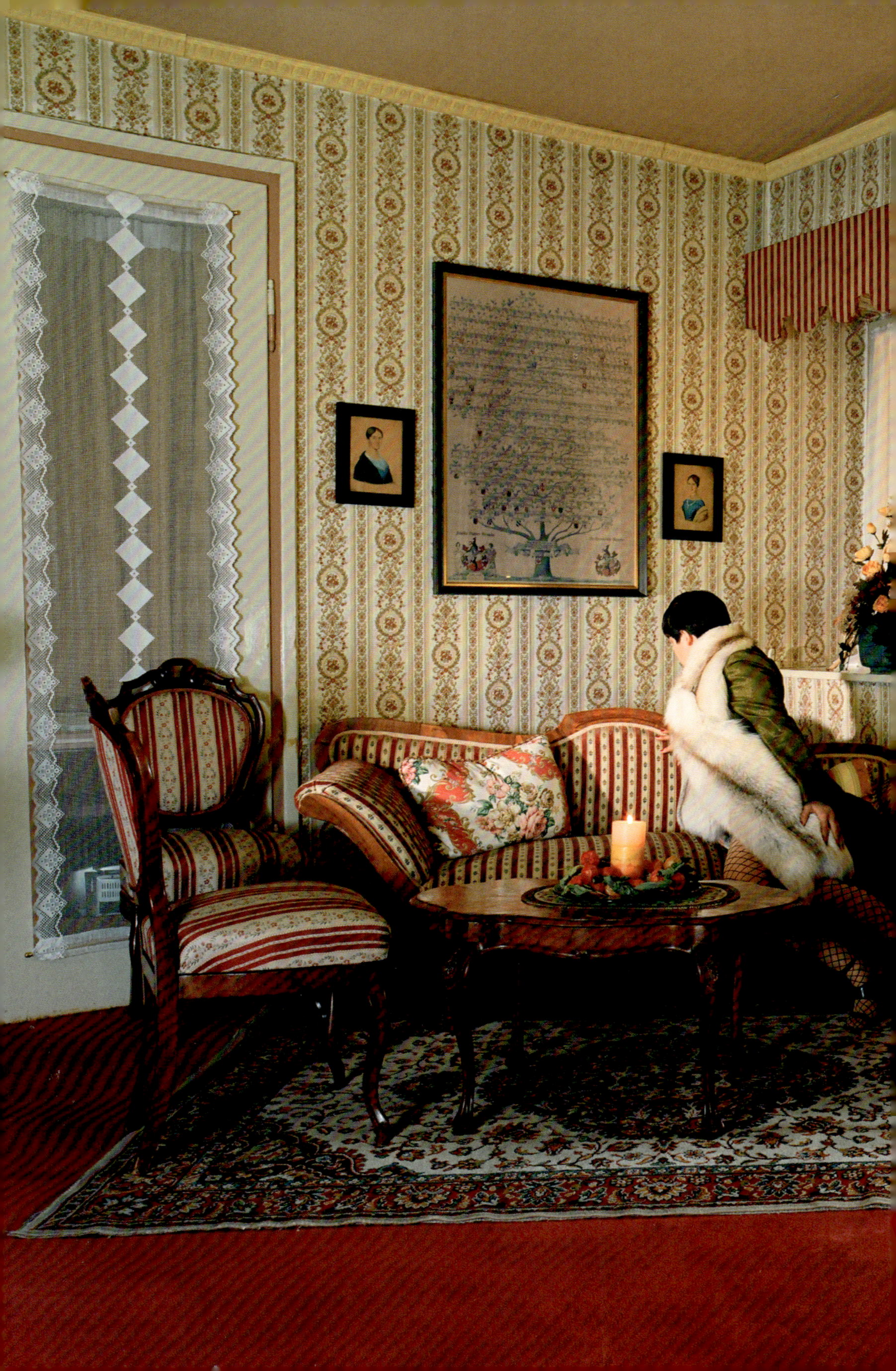

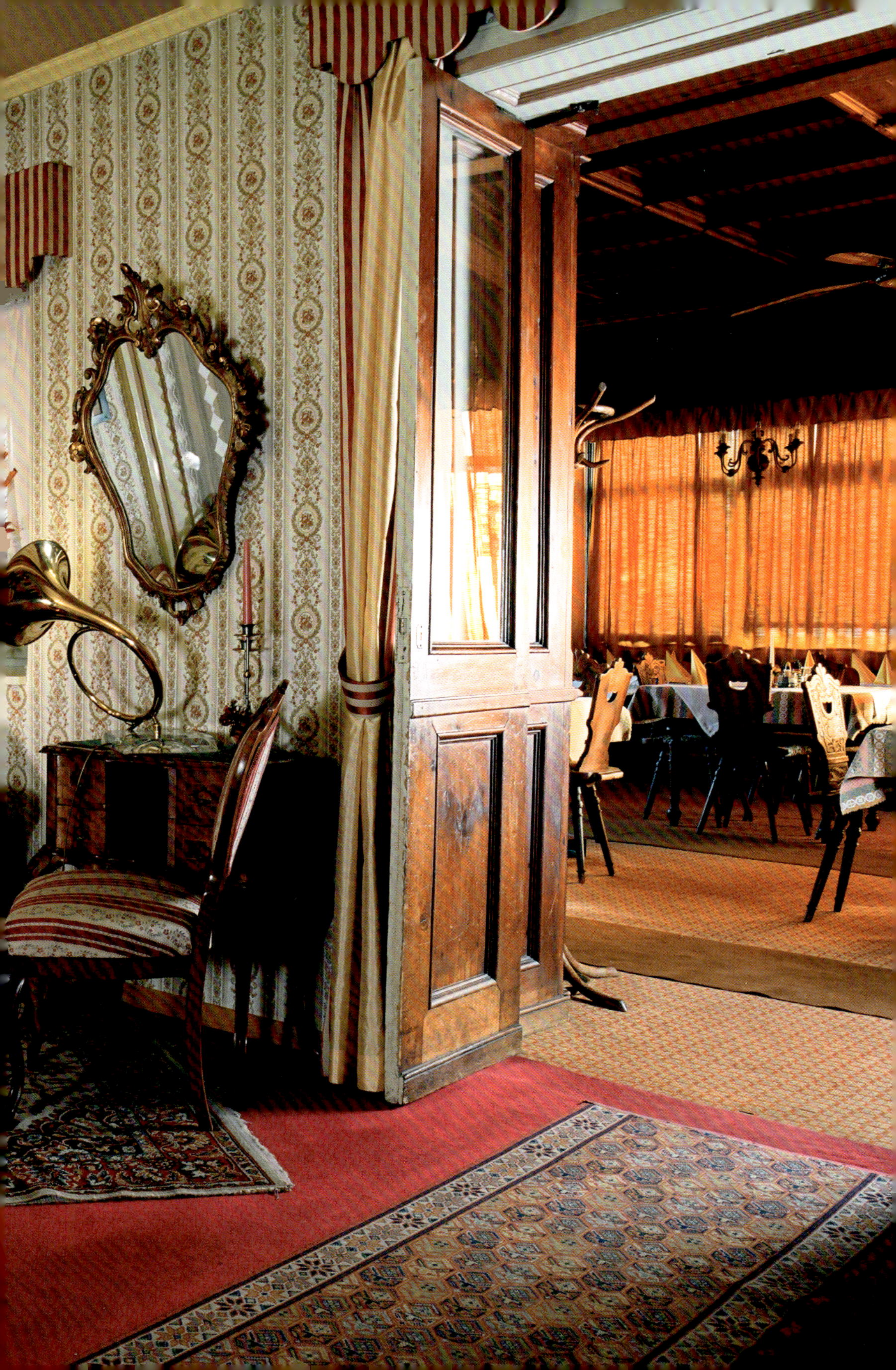

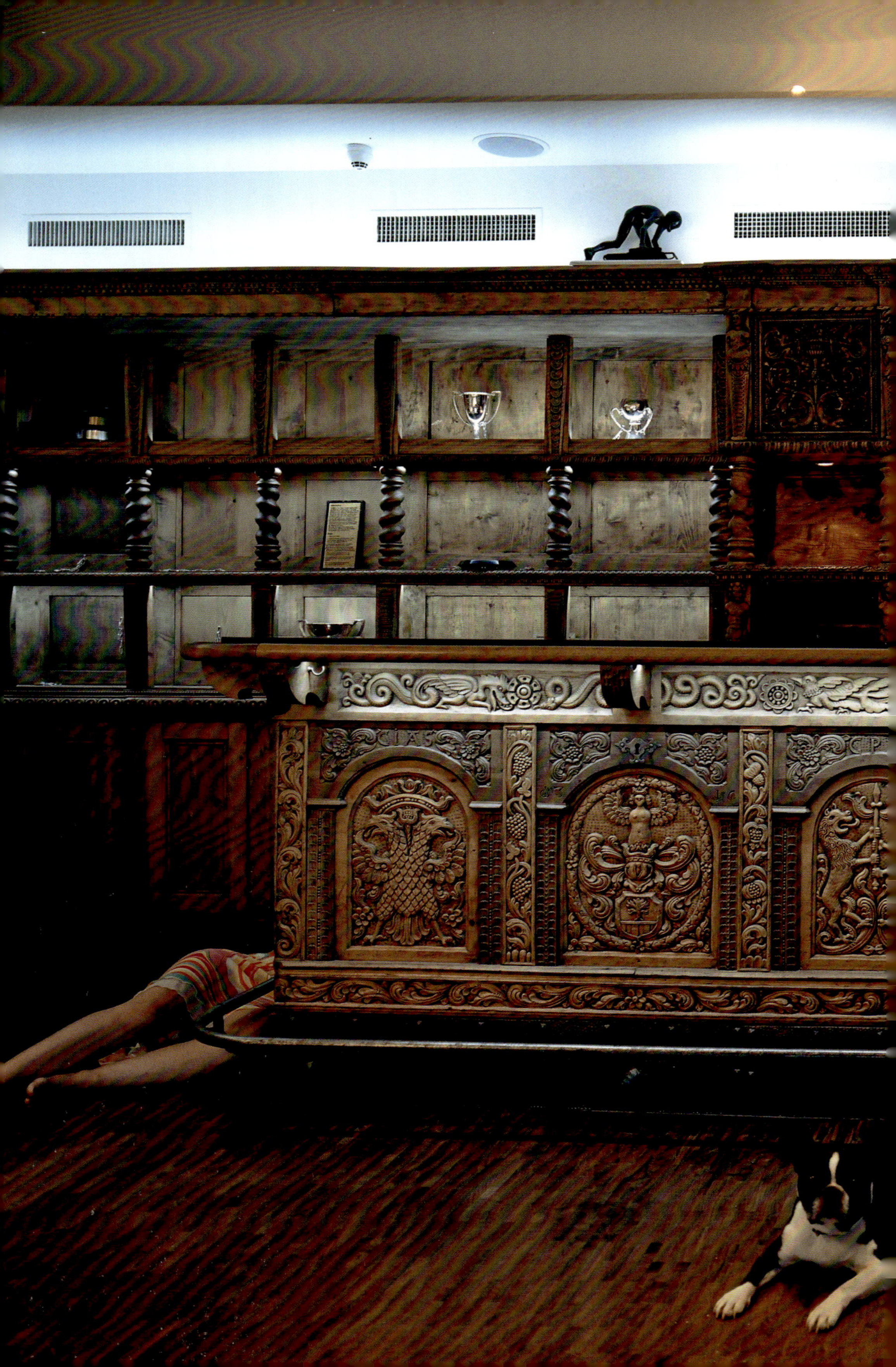

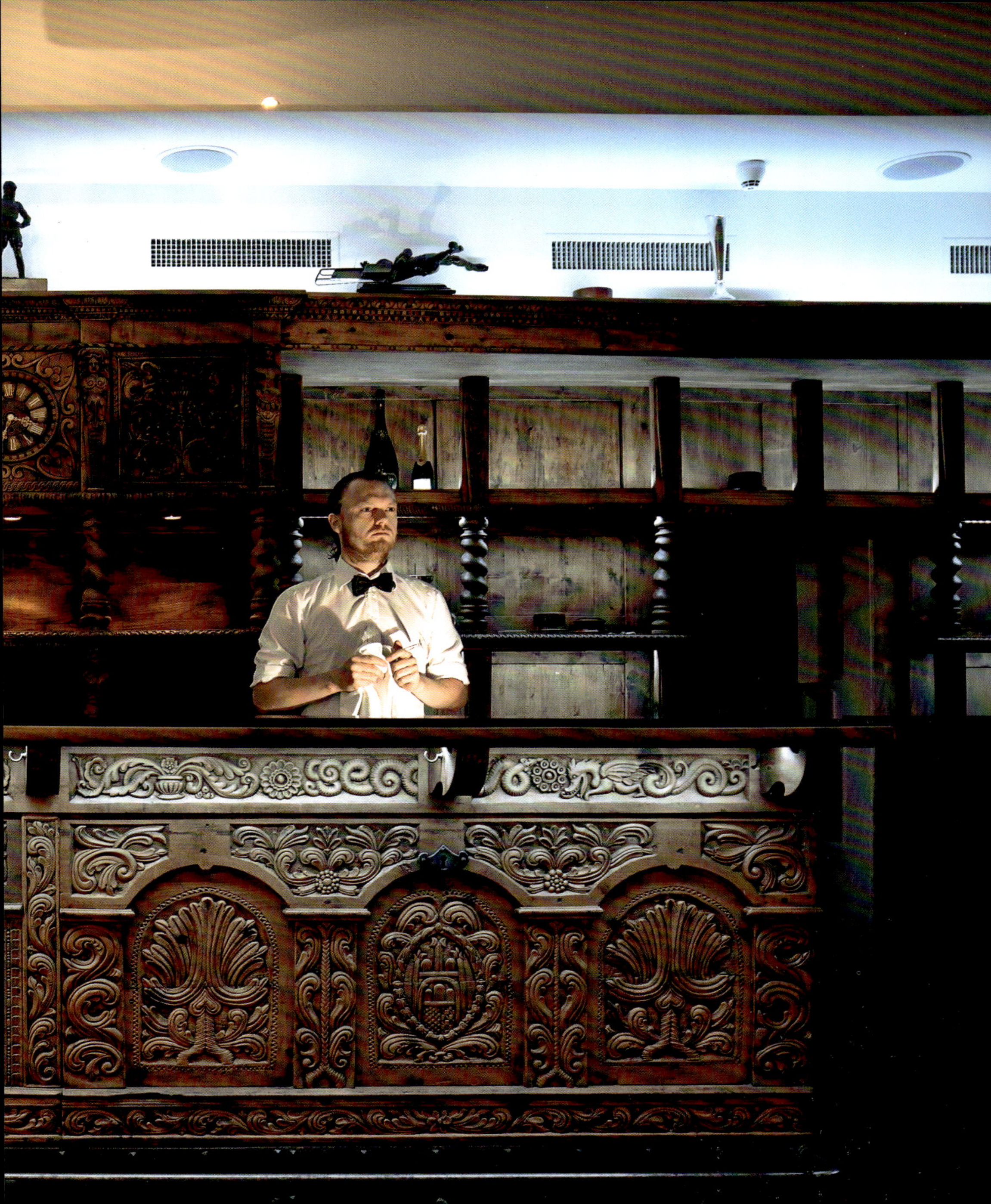

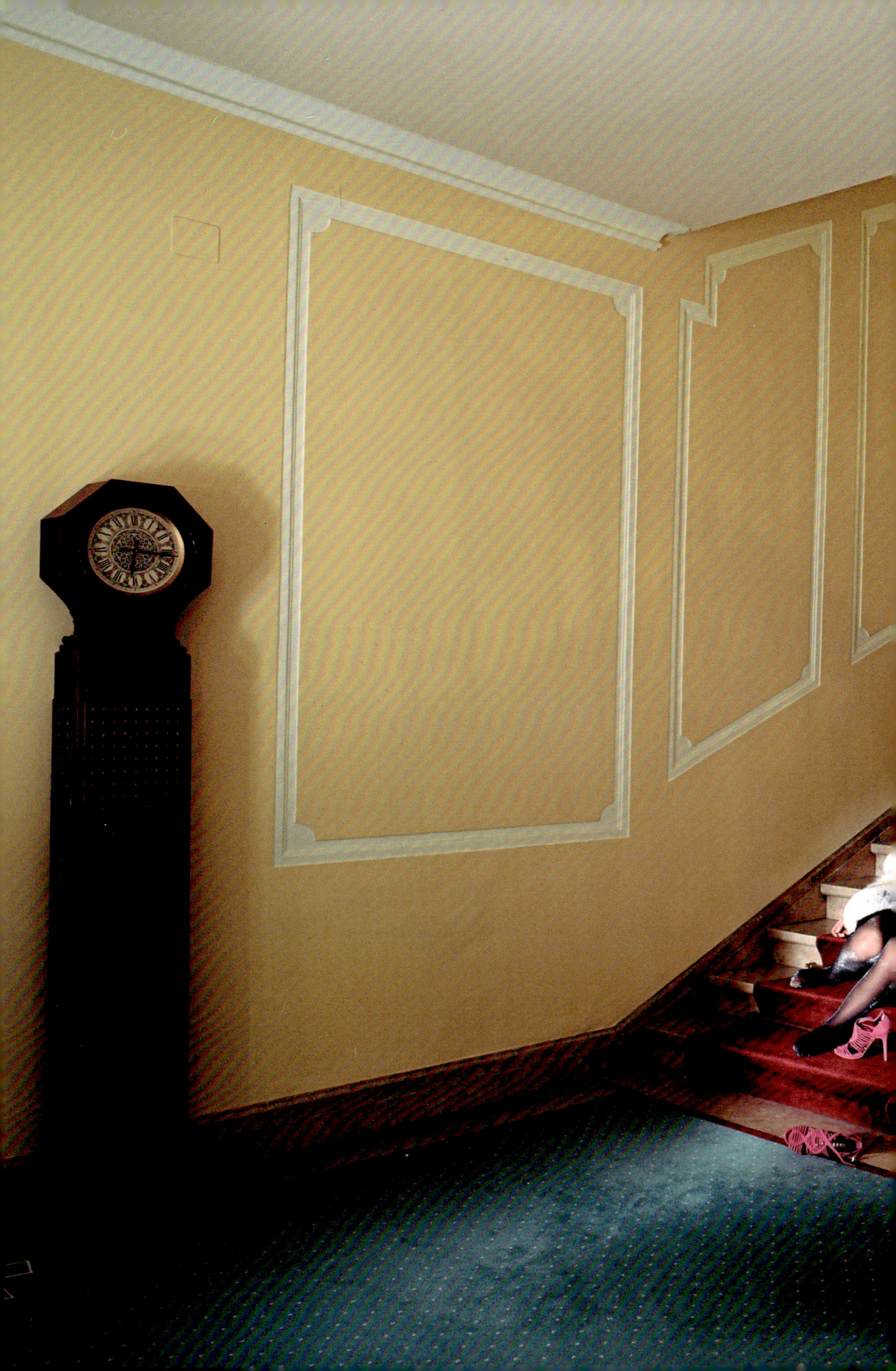

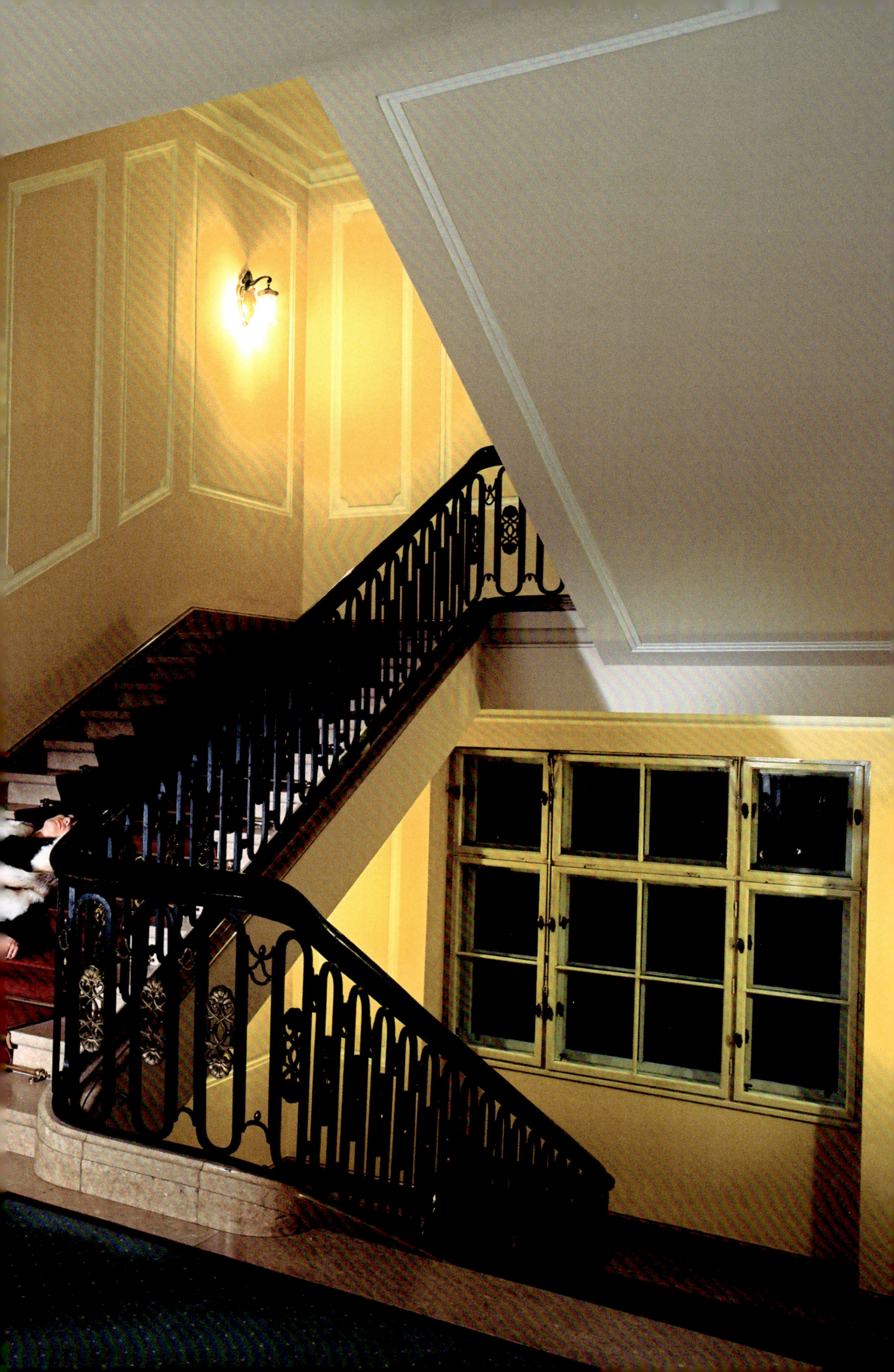

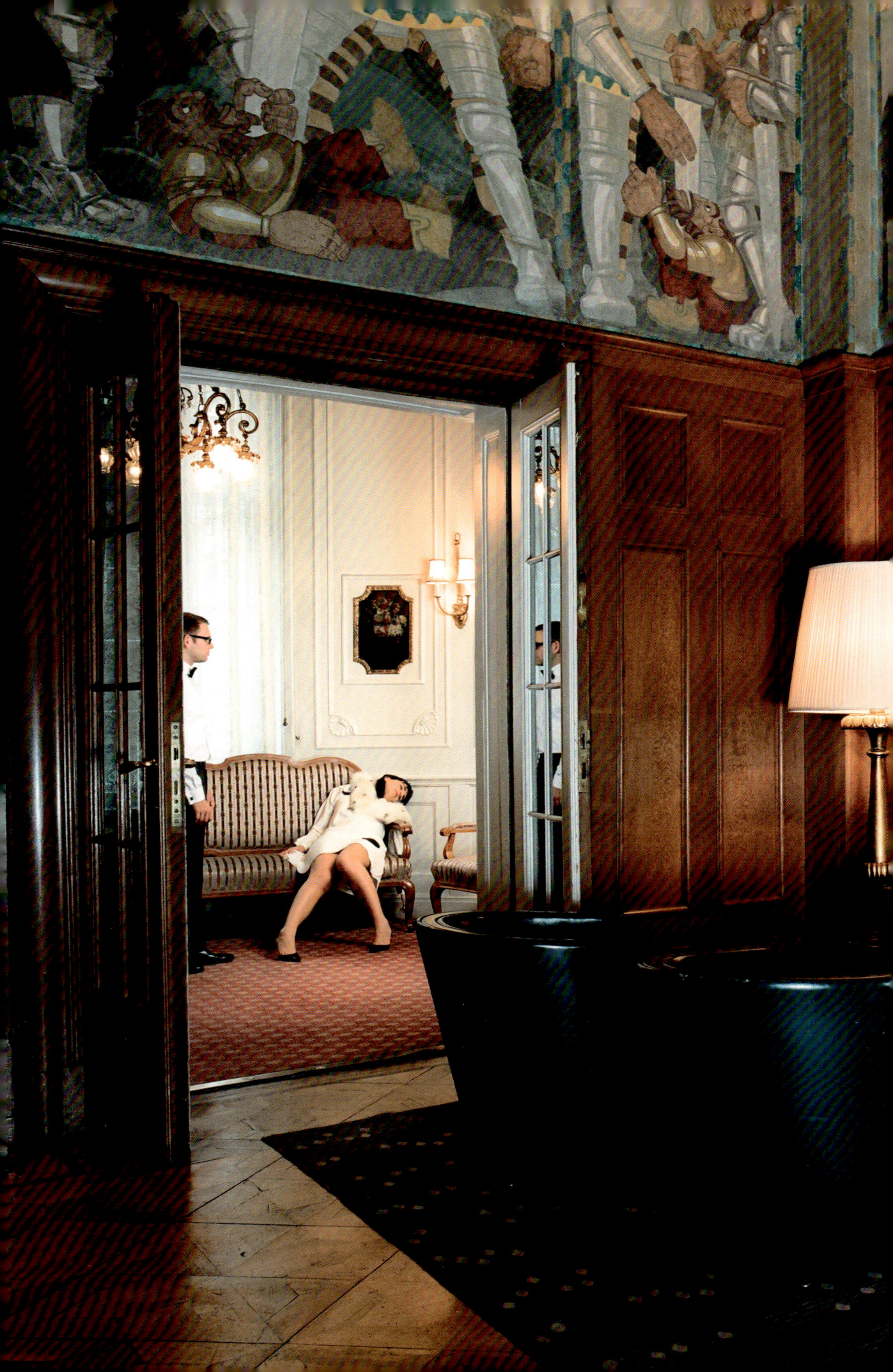

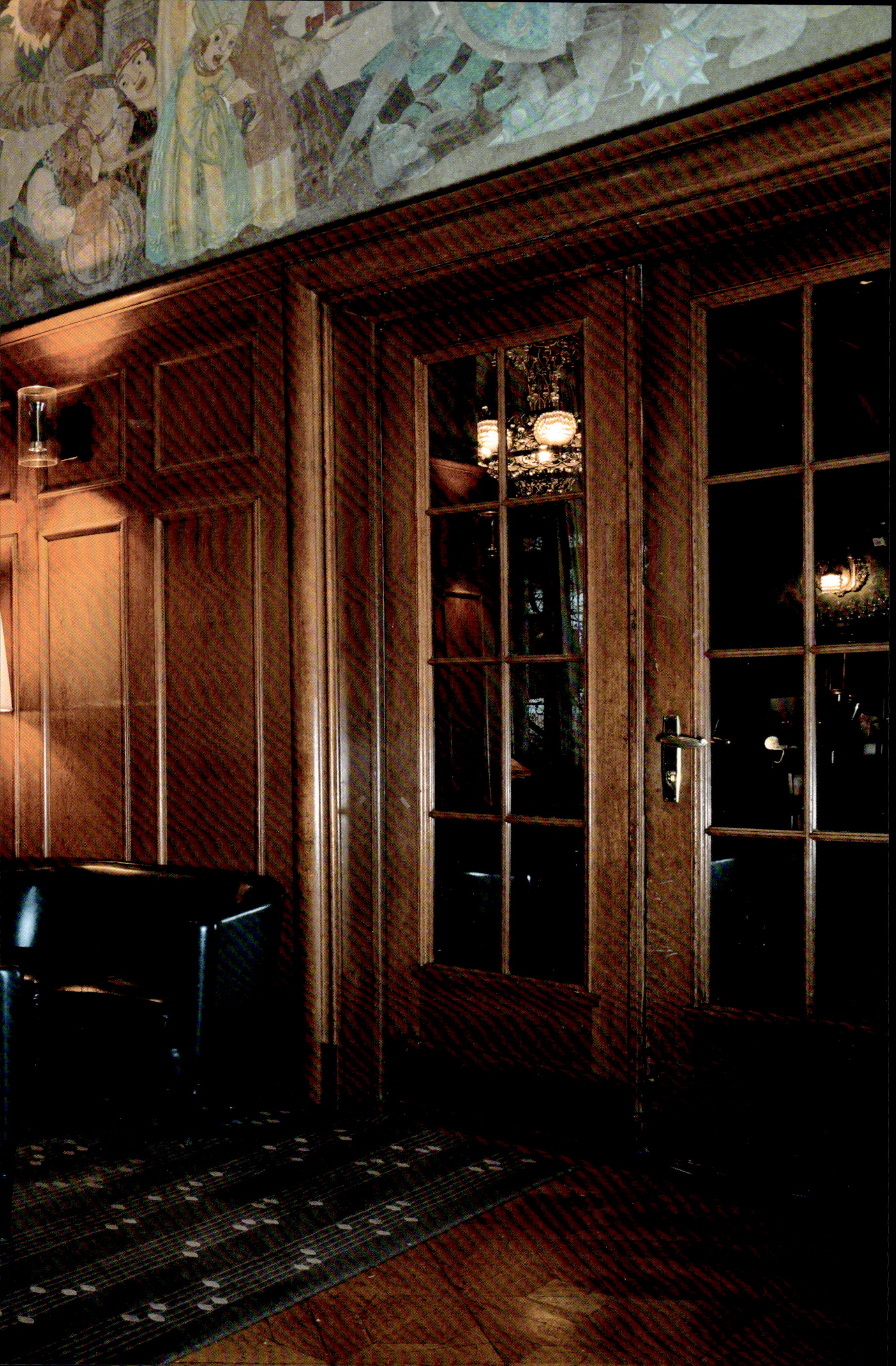

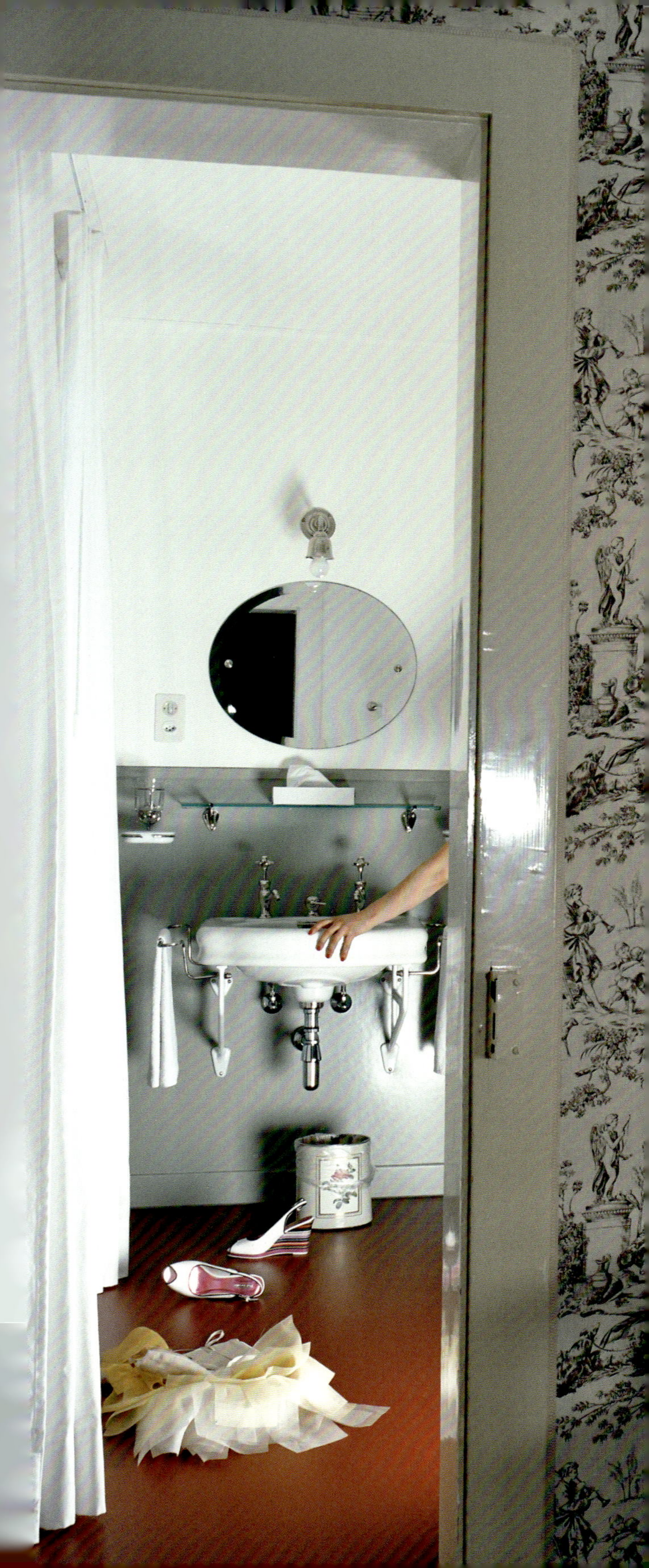

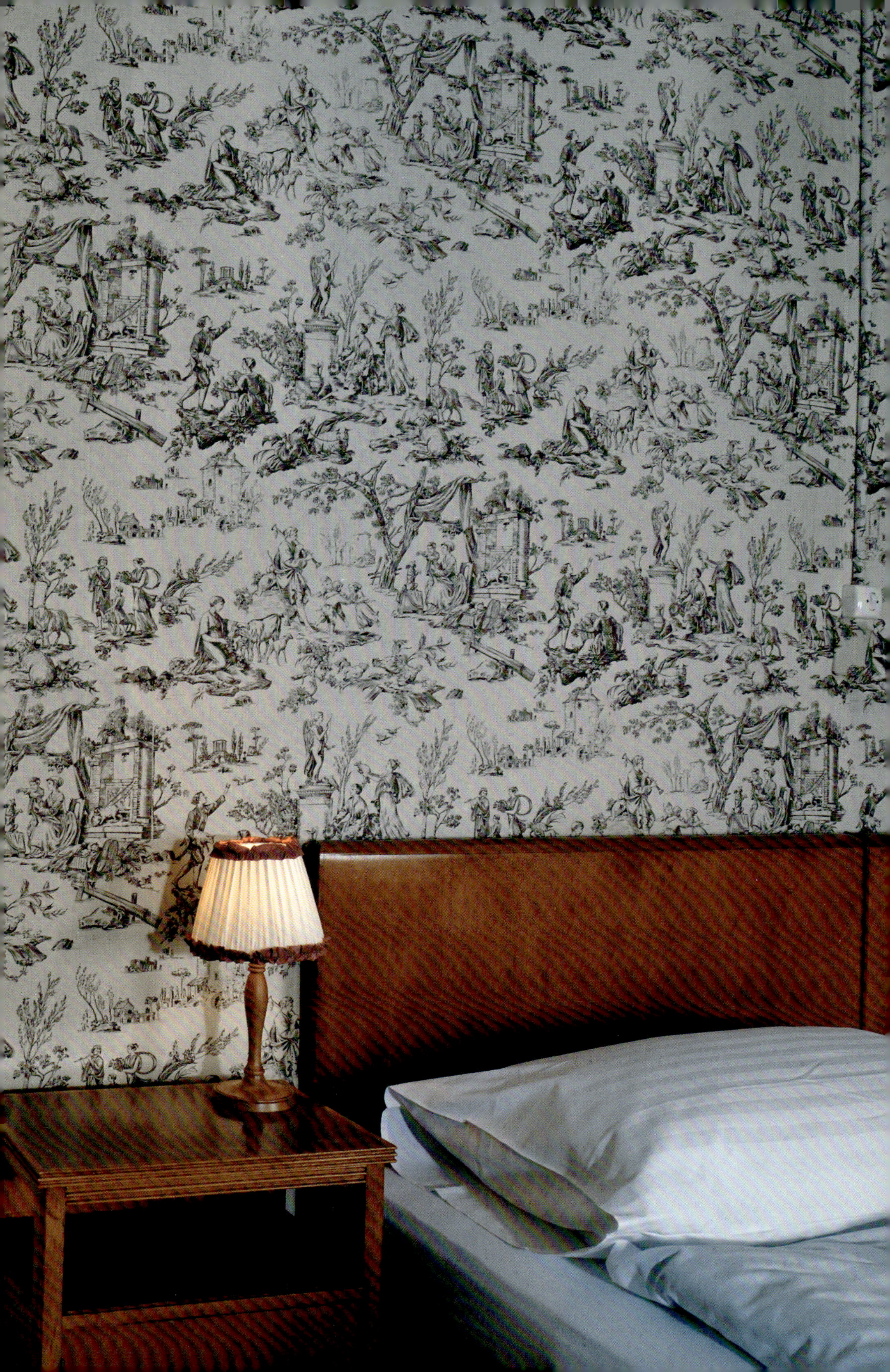

He crushed the slip of paper into a tiny ball with one hand and tossed it aside, not bothering to watch where it fell. He deliberately placed his glass on the sideboard and poured another.

"No," he said.

She moved to adjust the curtain, pulling first on the tasseled cord, and when that had no immediate effect, using the sharp heel of her shoe to dig and pull the heavy velvet to one side with small violence, revealing a narrow oblong slit of twilight, trees already black against a saturated sky of French blue, the color fading from light to dark like the nuances of fine enamel. Among the green silent bleat of rising fireflies, she could see the sporadic bend of flashlight beams between the trees, gaining mass as the night sucked away the blue-grey hues that lingered at the edge of the lawn, the veranda balustrade, a handful of gardening tools propped against the far wall, the curve of a child's pail forgotten in the grass.

She turned back into the room.

"Aren't you going to share?"

He brought the bottle from the sideboard and filled her outstretched glass, careful not to meet her eyes.

"No," he repeated.

"I didn't ask," she said, eyes fixed on the torque

of the fold of fabric pulled tight between his shoulder blades.

"You didn't have to," he said without turning.

Very slowly, almost languidly, she moved deliberately around the back of the sofa to take a seat at one end, her progress sending out tight ripples of energy that rebounded and collided against the walls and the furniture. He braced his hands against the sharp edge of the sideboard as if against a swell of water, head bucking back, rising for air. When he finally did turn, she could see a glimmer of sweat pearling on the high angle of his forehead.

She shook the ice in her glass.

"Don't be so dramatic," she said.

Out in the dark, the dogs began to bark in earnest, high plaintive yelps of discovery so intense that they were barely muffled by the thick velvet and double sashes of the conservatory windows. He was struck by how similar she looked to the way he had seen her that cold night in July, when she had thought that no one was looking; the sympathetic curve of her mouth was tight with something he would never be able to define, except that it made him feel like she belonged to him.

She placed a hand impulsively on her belly where the child moved. The sudden movement had

THE GARDENS

The main building is framed by two picturesque gardens that lead down to the only remaining Victorian greenhouse, a remnant of what was once a substantial park, before land was sold off over the years as the property changed hands and subsequent owners fell victim to the treacherous tides of games of chance, unhappy marriages, shady investments, or simple bad luck. The greenhouse itself has been left in its found condition, with the exception of necessary structural reinforcement, and excavation on the site has unearthed sherds of early native pottery, a wartime tin box filled with papers, a talisman believed to be of Celtic origin, and several fragments of unidentified bone, thought to be animal remains from a previous structure that was located on the site. These items can be viewed by appointment in the private museum located in the OLD MILL (see map).

With the aid of photographs and documents from the local historical society, the west garden has been reconstructed to prewar conditions. The assortment of rare rose types is exemplary, including a stunning example of the *Lady Pearl*–a prize-winning bloom named after the second owner's wife, a noted beauty in her day. Look for it on your left as you pass the marble sundial in the shape of a fish's tail. The collection of lupine and red bee balm attracts a variety of butterflies, including the rare Karner Blue butterfly, which was at one time prolific in this part of the country. The reseeding of native wild blue lupine, wild lily of the valley and certain types of loosestrife has encouraged the return of these seldom seen insects. There is a colorful collection of Oriental and Asiatic lilies in the east garden, reached when following the path through the original kitchen garden, home to culinary and medicinal herbs of all types and particularly fragrant in the morning hours. Note the large granite trough at the far end of the path, a naturally occurring formation put to good use by the addition of a hand-operated water pump installed by one of the building's earliest owners.

The house has been at times private residence, sport club, hotel, and barracks*, and was rumored to have been the site of a brothel, though no concrete evidence to the fact has ever surfaced during the renovation or extensive research undertaken by the property's current owner.

For more information on the main house, please see Chapter 3.

*Recent restoration on north side of the greenhouse has uncovered a series of crude graffiti and propagandist slogans, including a traditional peeping Tom figure with the underlying caption "Kilroy was Here." These are believed to have been left by soldiers who quartered here during the long winter of '44.

HISPANO-SUIZA 1922 H6B

Named for the dual parentage of its founder, the Hispano-Suiza Automobile Company is known for having created the most exclusive and advanced luxury passenger vehicles of its day. The H6 was one of the most produced models; it is estimated that 2,500 were made between its introduction at the 1919 Paris Automobile Salon and the close of the company in 1938. The straight six engine of this luxury passenger vehicle was inspired by the work its designer, Marc Birkigt, did on aircraft engines. With the addition of an overhead camshaft, it is in essence half of Birkigt's V12 design, featuring screwed steel liners and water passages that were enameled to prevent corrosion. The 3 speed manual transmission controlled a 6.5 liter engine capable of producing 135 horsepower, placed in front and powering the rear wheels, achieving top speeds of 85 mph. The four-wheel brakes, with 16 inch aluminum drums with cast-in steel liners, was later used by Rolls Royce under patent and was unique for its time.

Only the chassis was produced by the company. After completion, it was delivered to a custom coach builder for assembly, with the result that every automobile produced was unique in appearance. The model depicted is thought to have been produced not in the original Paris factory, but in the Czech Republic. The origins of the interior is unknown, but the Dual Cowl Phaeton design would indicate coachwork from the Brunn Company of Buffalo, New York. The seat squabs are of dark blue leather, trimmed with oxblood leather piping. The body is sky blue with dark blue mud guards and cherry wood trim. The serial number is illegible, however as H-S autos were some most expensive automobiles produced at the time, possible owners would have been limited to a small number of privileged individuals.

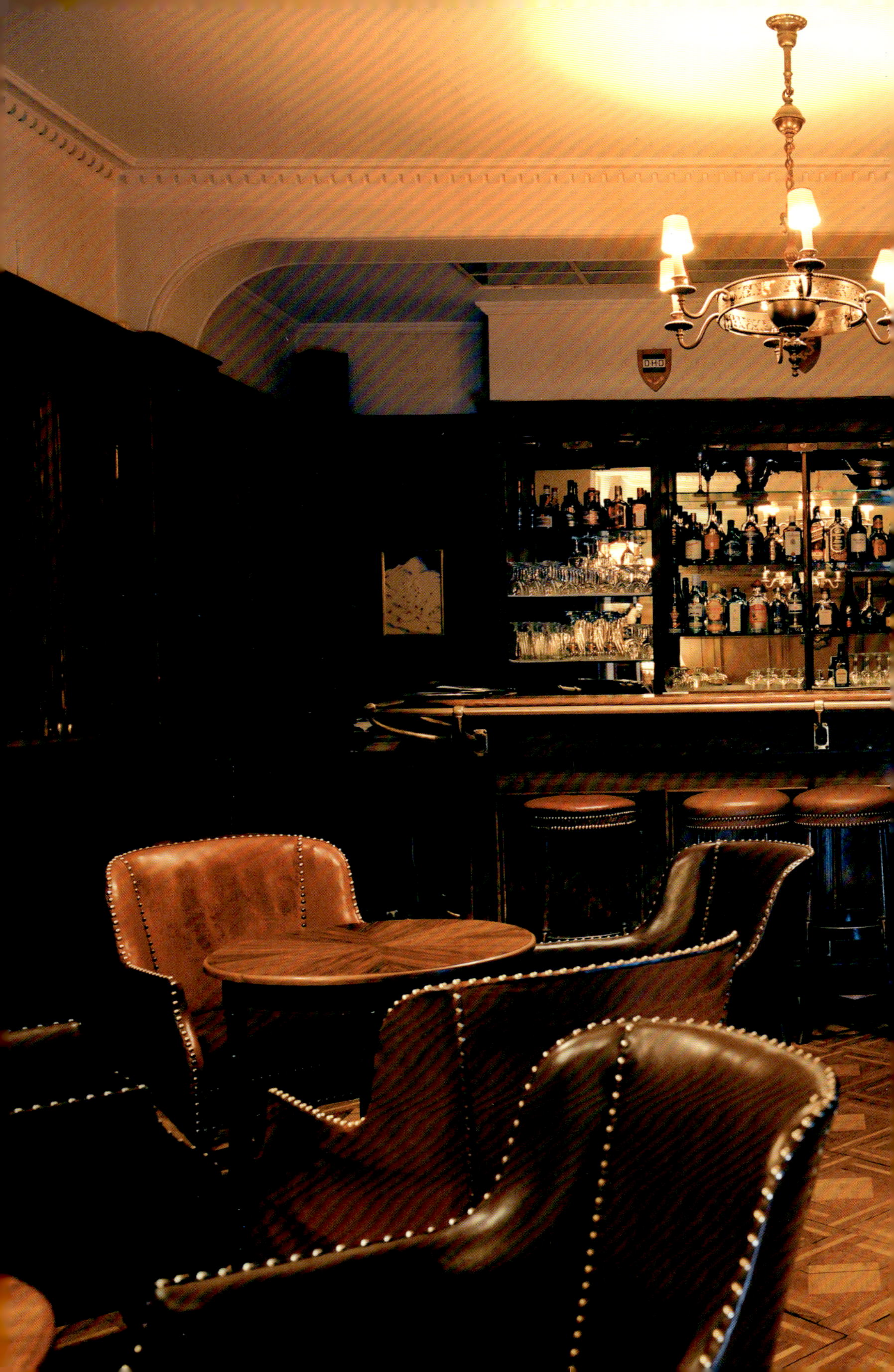

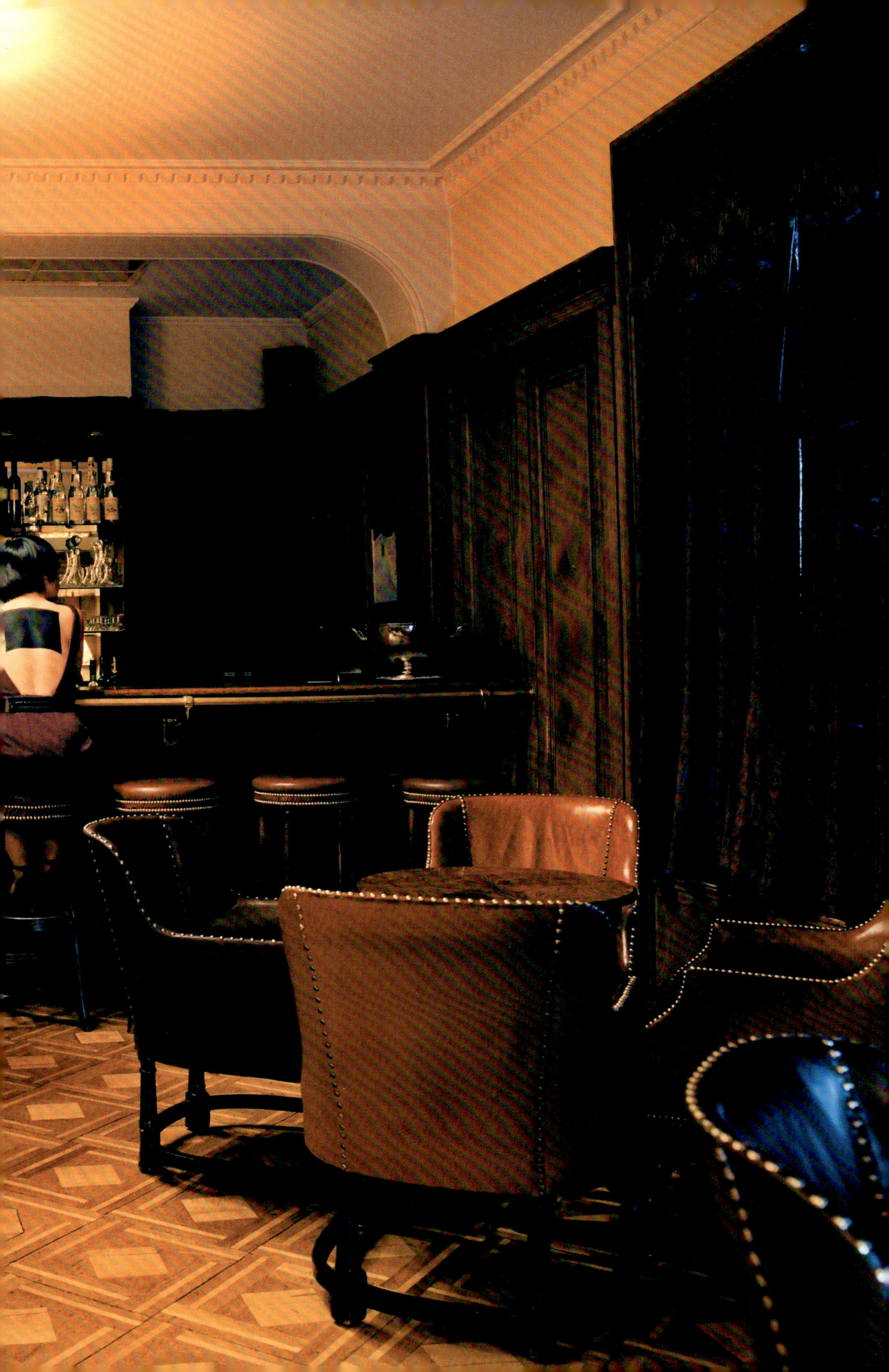

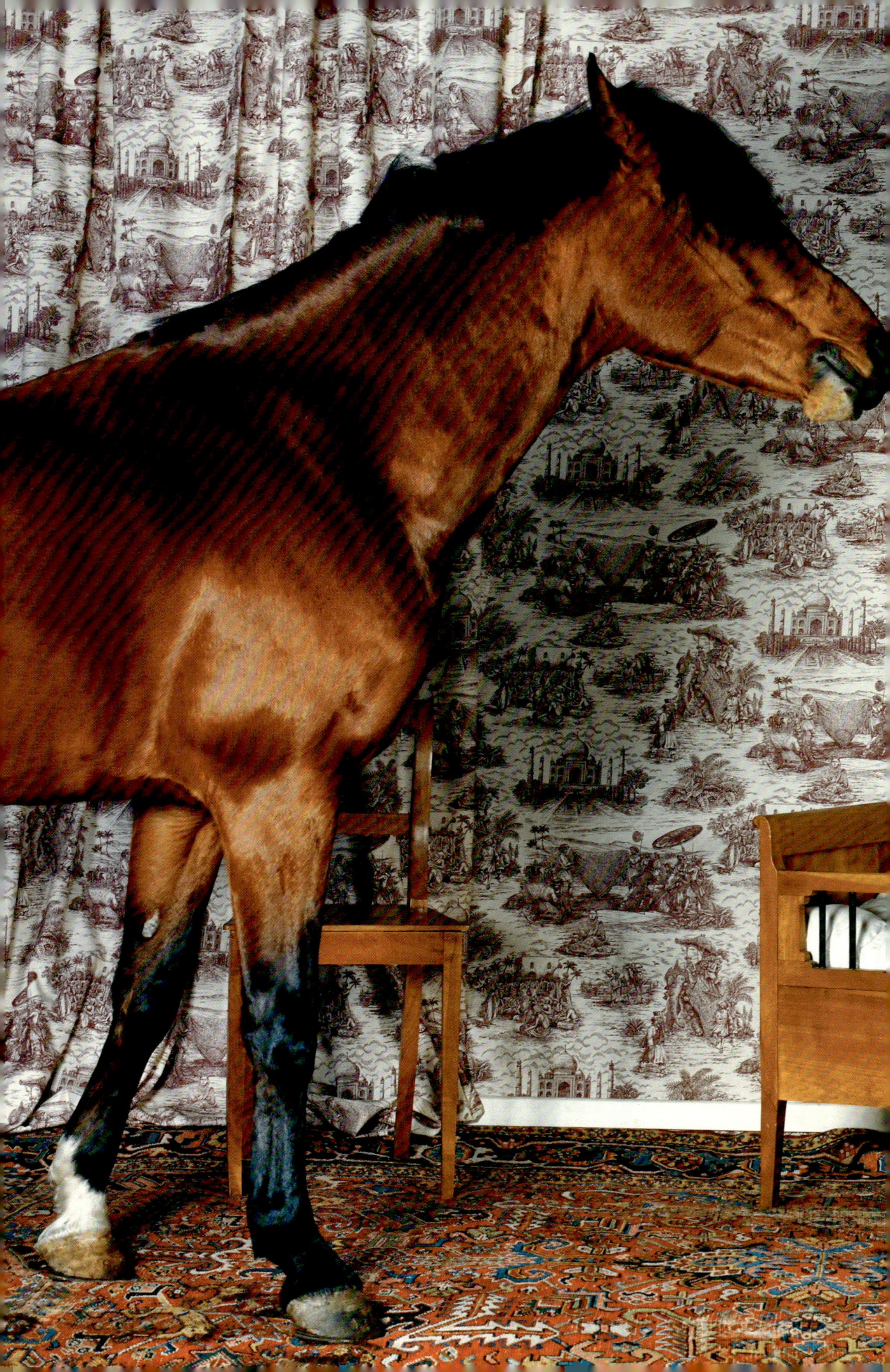

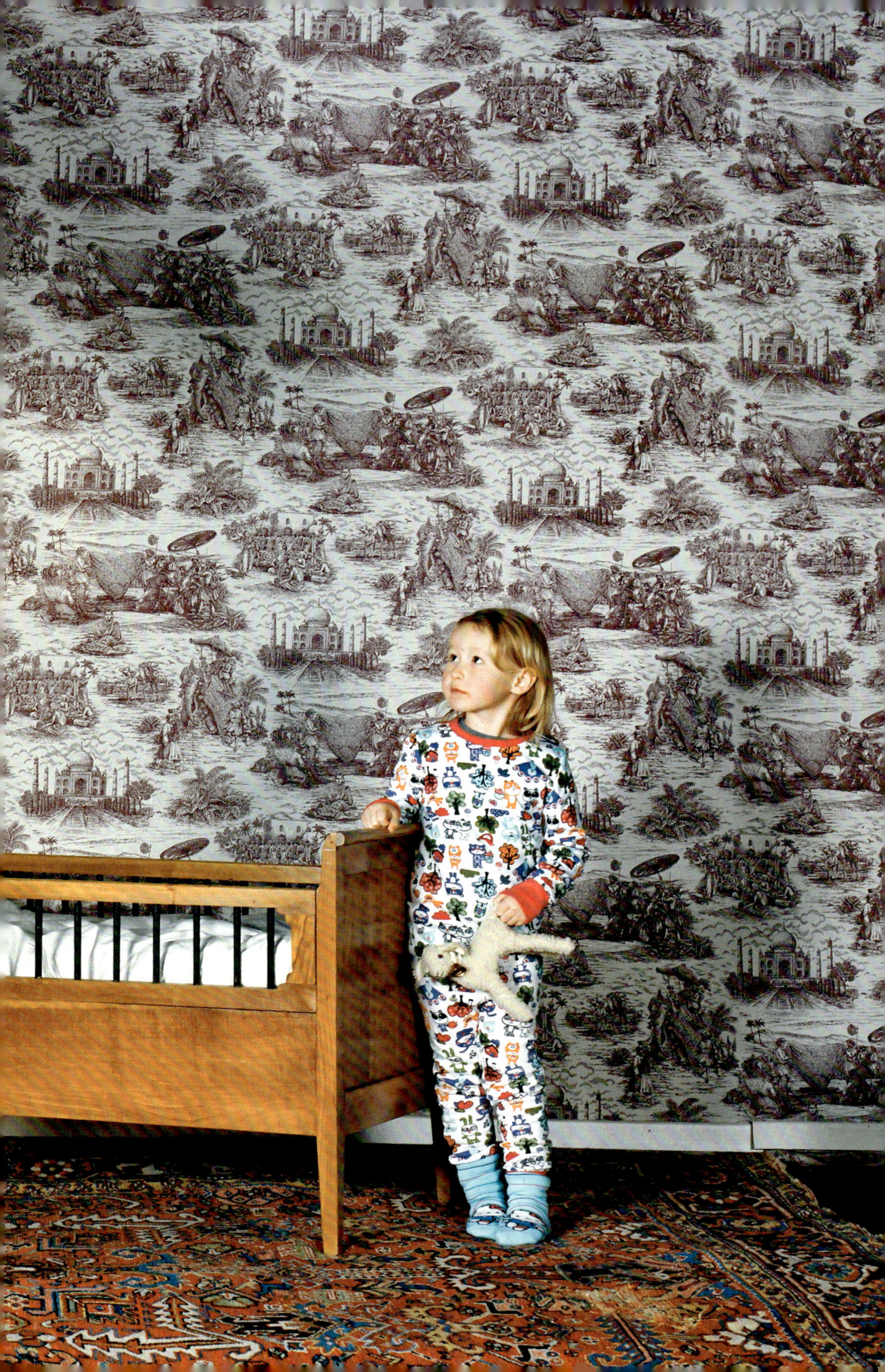

VIII

She was the only one seated at the bar, one foot stable on the rail and the other thrust out into space, held there like a bodily satellite by the aggressive angle of her crossed legs. There were dim lights, the curves of glass, her image appropriated and overwritten by the coy advertising slogans etched on the mirror propped behind the bar.

She eyed the stack of hotel brochures that lay fanned at her elbow as she sipped her drink. The influence of alcohol made a wondrous blue temple out of the word "Hotel," the peaks of the letters quivering like the heart of a gas flame, "Deluxe" split in two like a metal spoon holding the gelatinous golden yolk of a quail egg, "Moroccan Delight" a cold studded brick red that faded into faceted black. More vivid as she focused on the fine print: "Pool"–hot pink shiny like lacquer, "Afternoon Delight"–the palest yellow of frothed vanilla malt, poured on black skin, "Monday Madness"– two slashes of grey green and black joined as violently as upraised swords. The prose was dizzying, nearly unreadable, letters swirling together like thick streams of paint. "Hotel", the word that appeared most often, seemed burned on the reverse side of her lids when she pressed her eyes closed, a small mass of blue luminescent bubbles percolating through milky white.

The bartender caught her attention with words like beige haze.

She nodded and watched him make her another drink, heard a couple enter from behind, their conversation veering between light and dark as she listened in, the woman's voice like the pink spiked petals of a three-day-old chrysanthemum, the man's like blue-black water. When they spoke over each other, their voices overlapped into a curious vibrant indigo, weaving in and out like the coils of a benign serpent in accidental harmony. They were in love, she decided, but not newly in love—something between pleasure and contentment vibrated from their words and painted the air around them like smoke.

The bartender came back, placed the drink before her and said something vaguely green.

She nodded again and took a slow pull.

At the request (iron grey) of the couple, the barman turned on the old dial radio and a voice pulsed through that sang something the color of warm pliant flesh, the color she knew she would speak

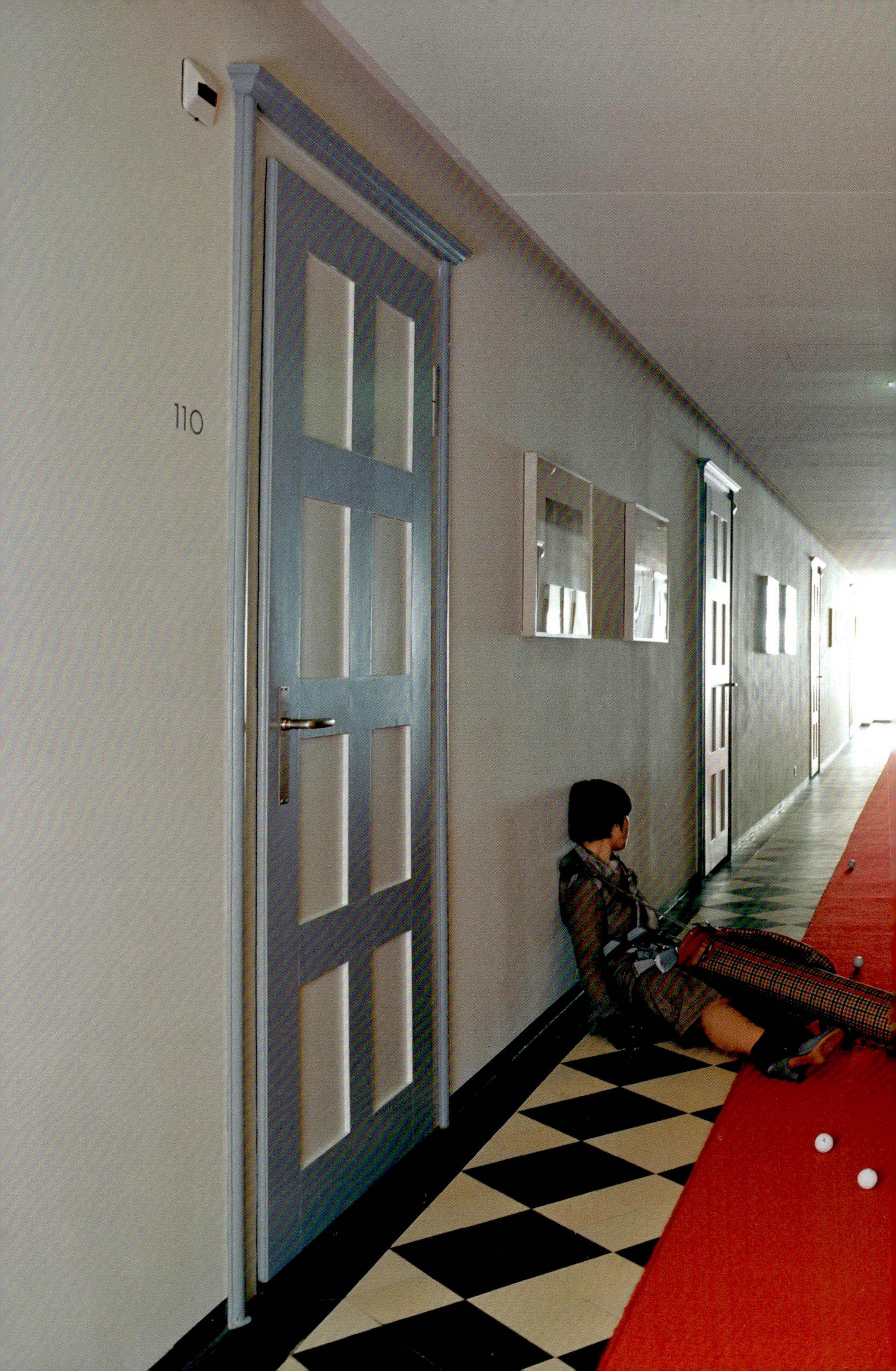
110

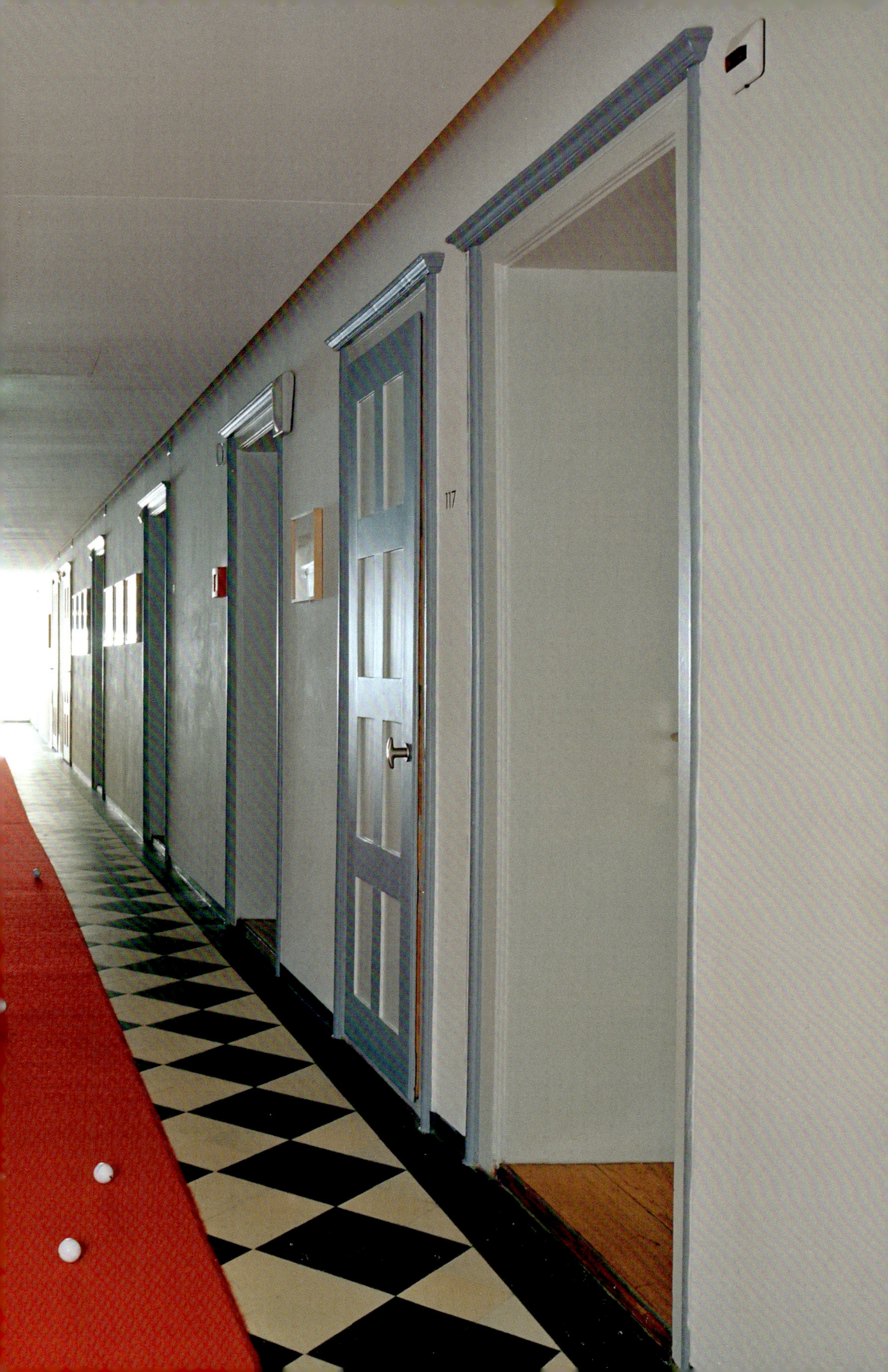
117

5:19 pm (Slow 6/8)

Bars of a Cage
Bars of a Cage
The light through my window
like through Bars of a Cage.

Like the tail of a dragon,
the smoke curls high
from all of the cigarettes
I've lit against the sky.

And all of my memories
Like ships on the sea,
They are loved by no one,
but they are loved by me.

Bars of a Cage
Bars of a Cage
Love that surrounds me
like Bars of a Cage.

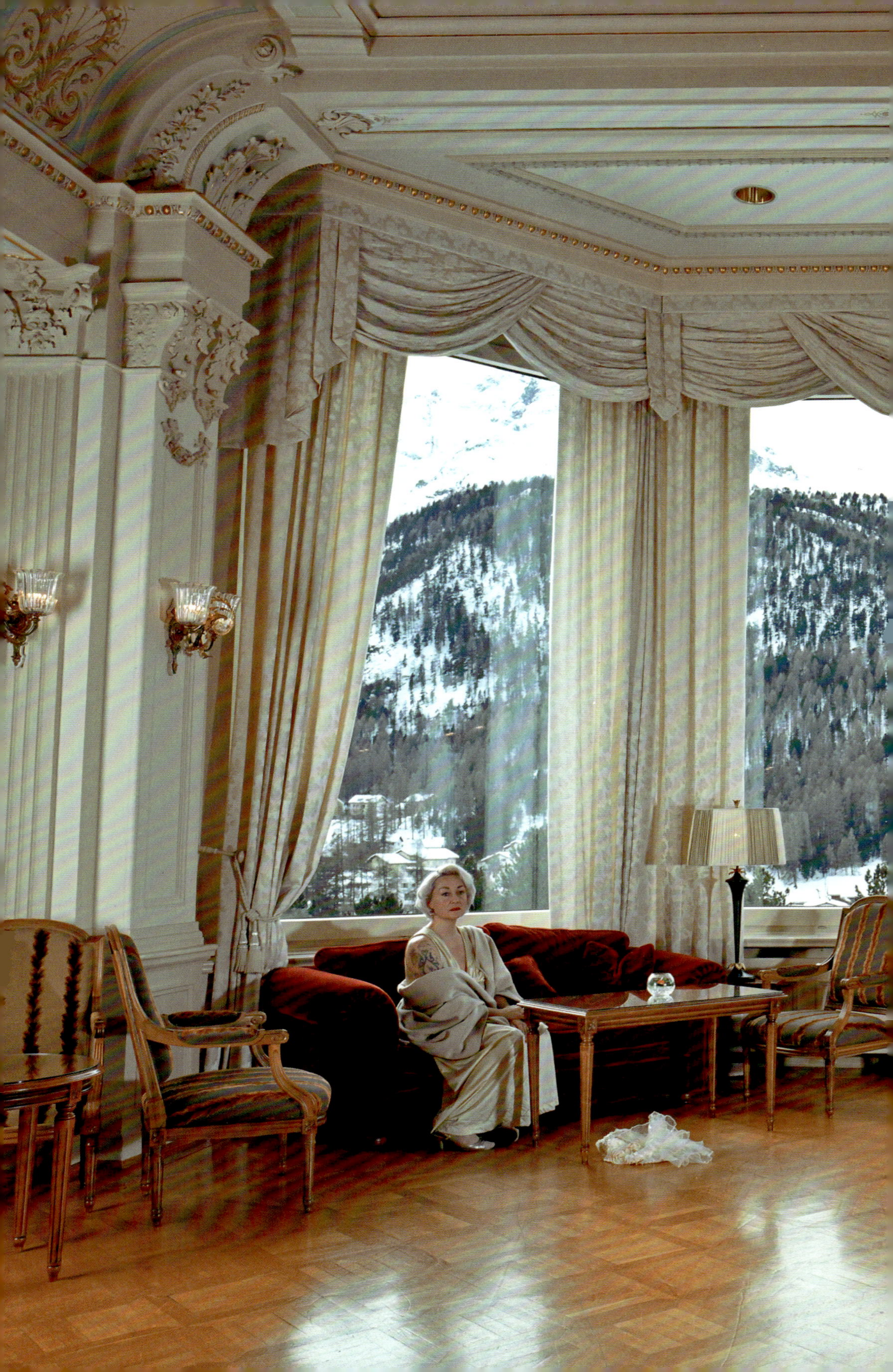

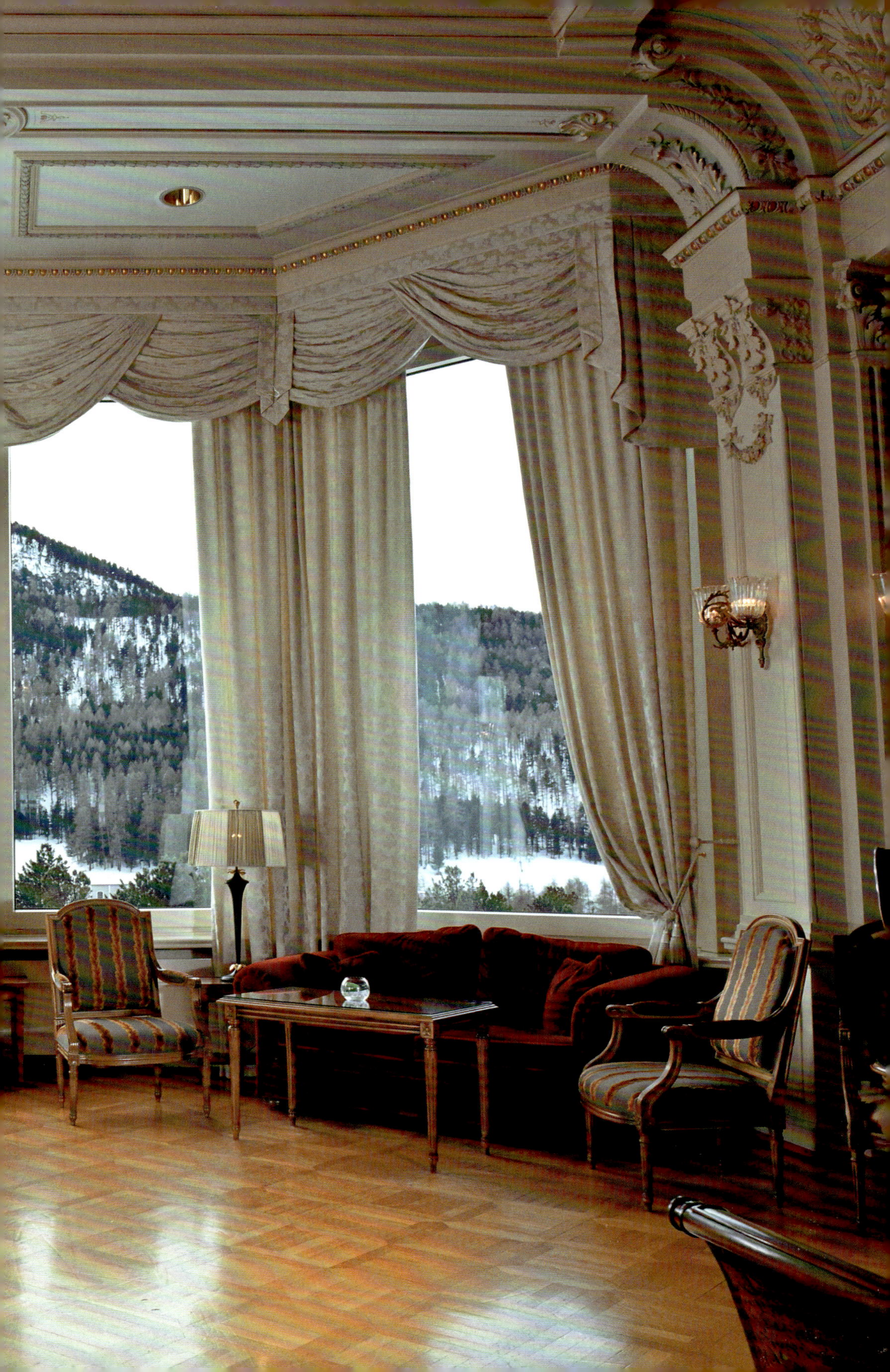

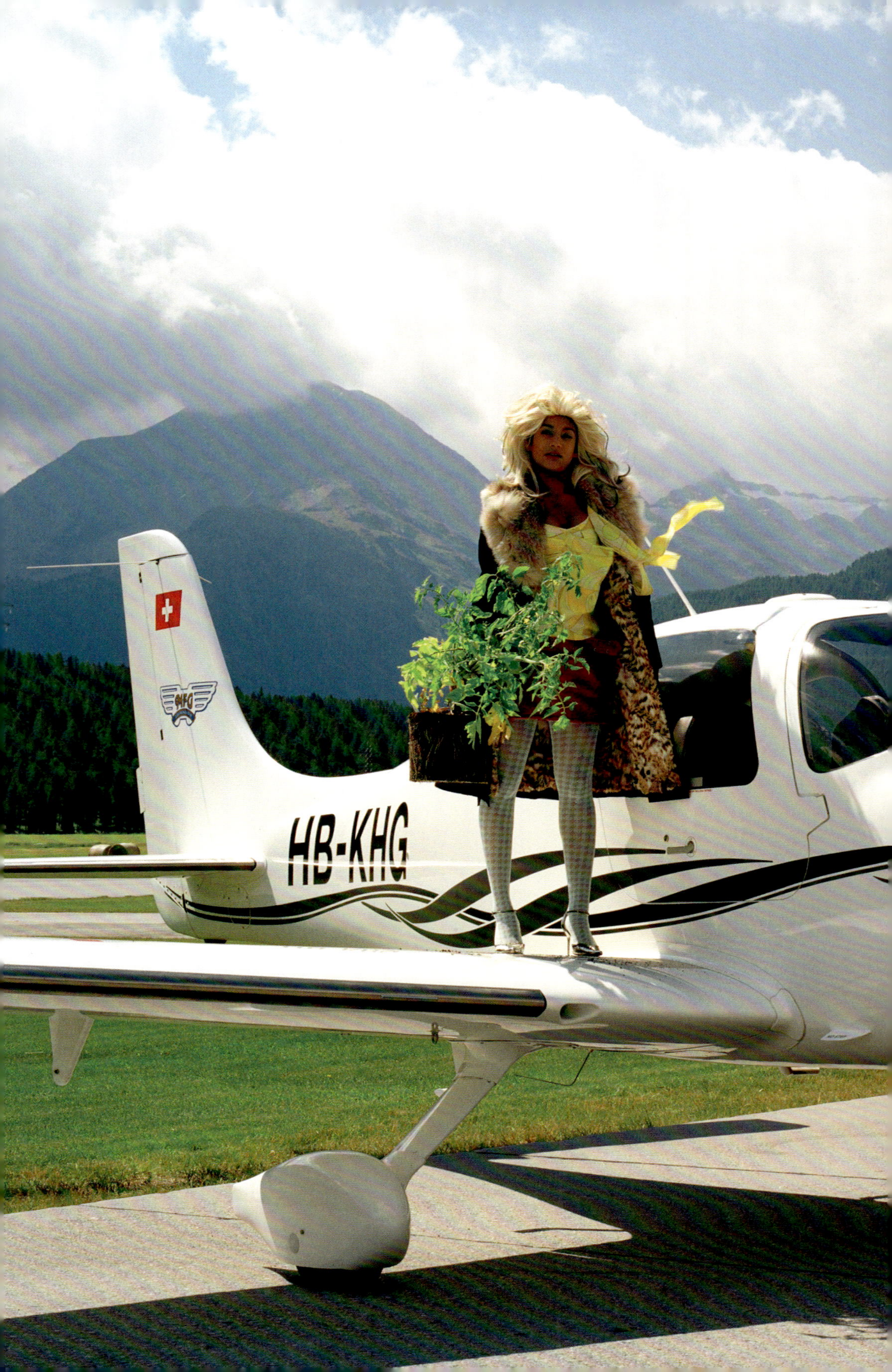

HB-KHG

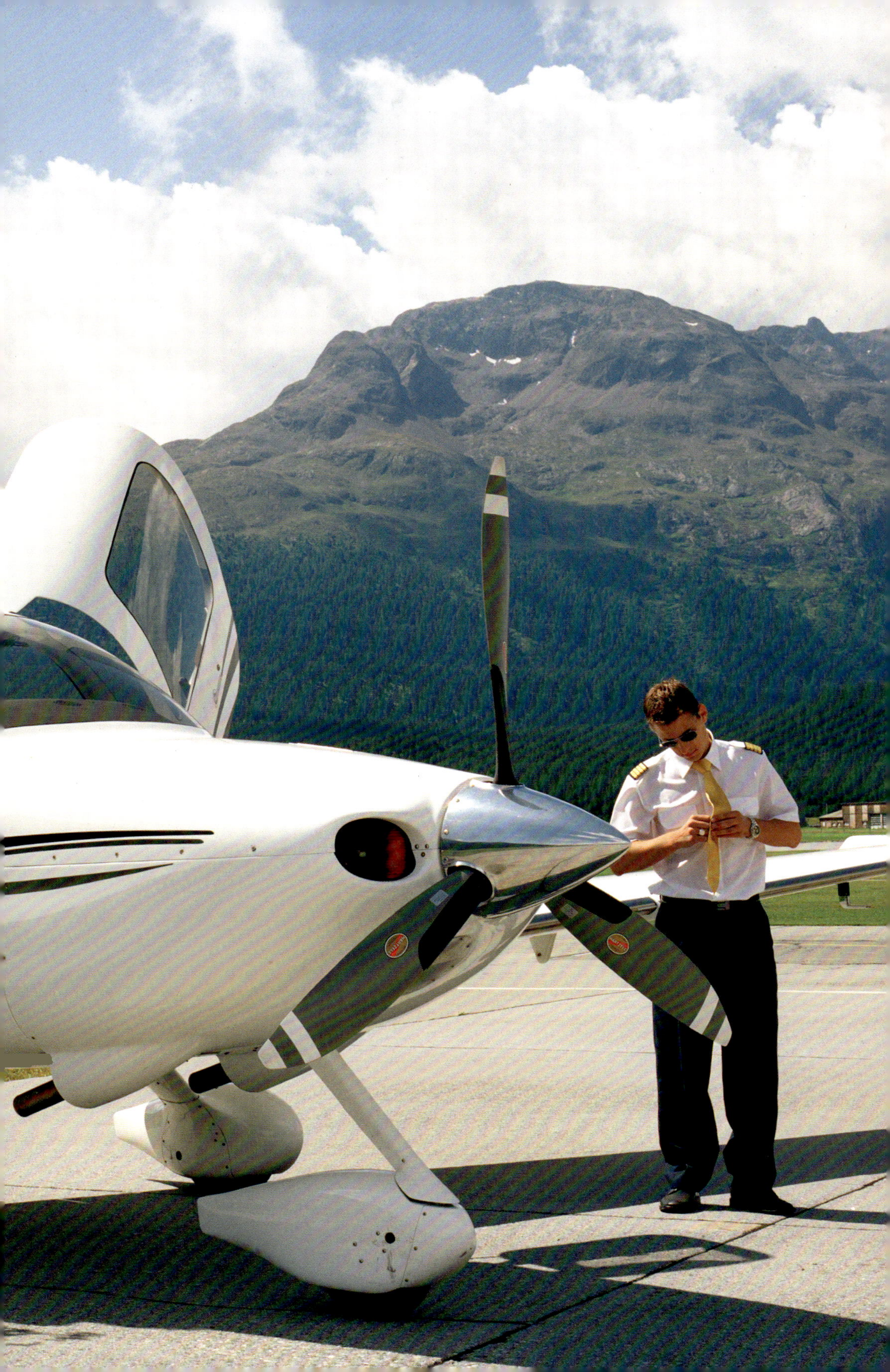

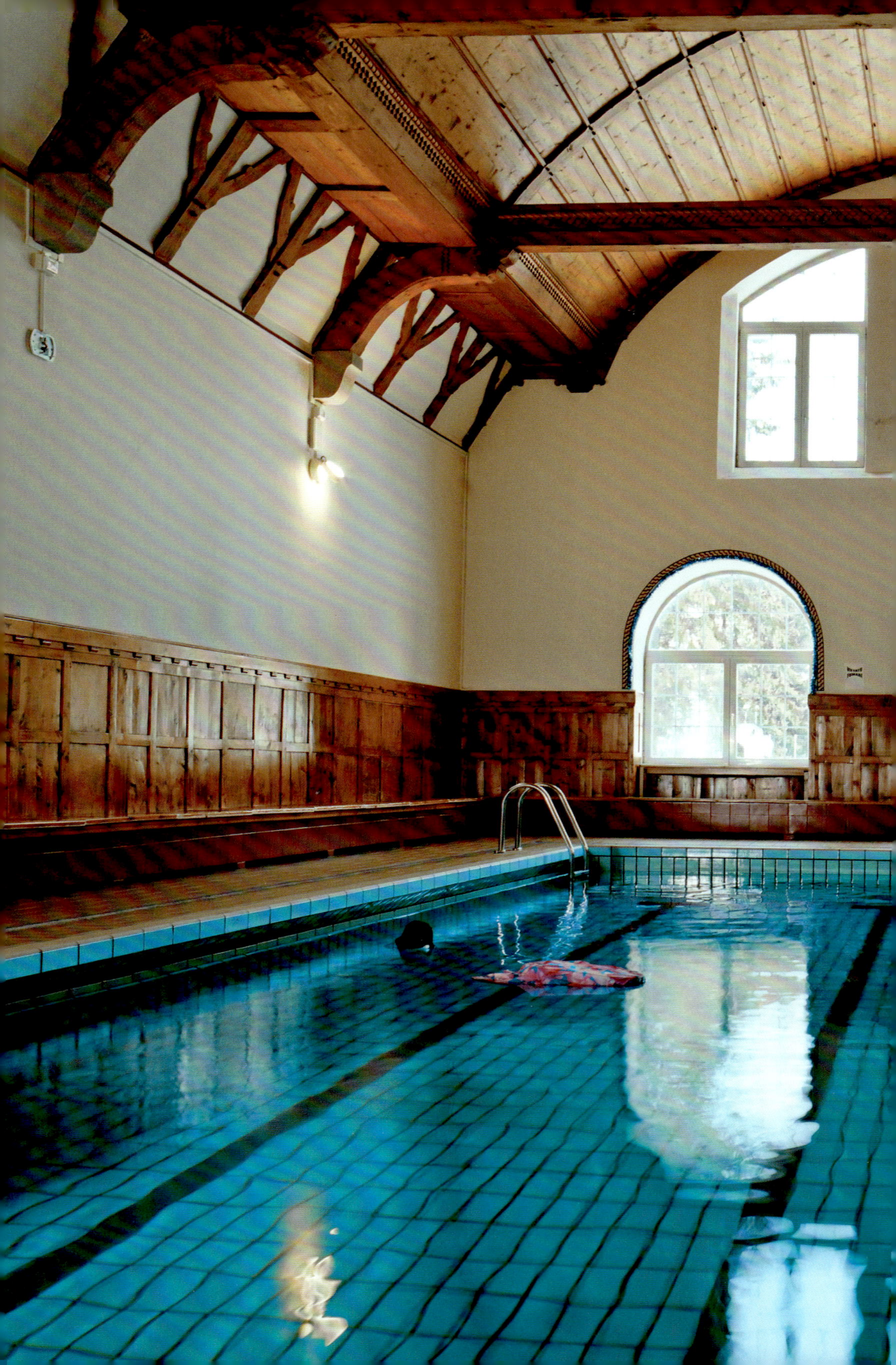

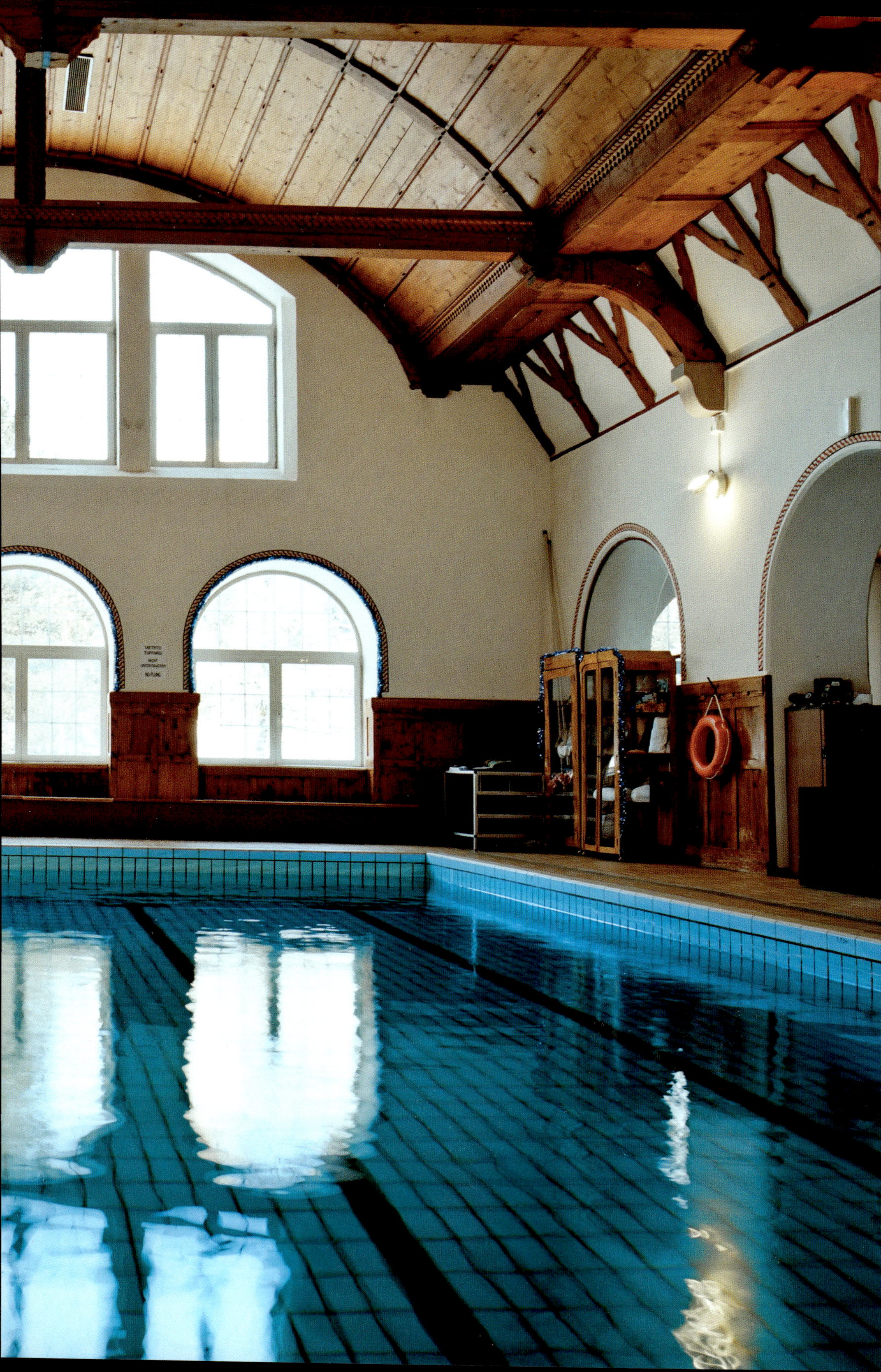

VIETATO
TUFFARSI
NICHT
UNTERTAUCHEN
NO DIVING

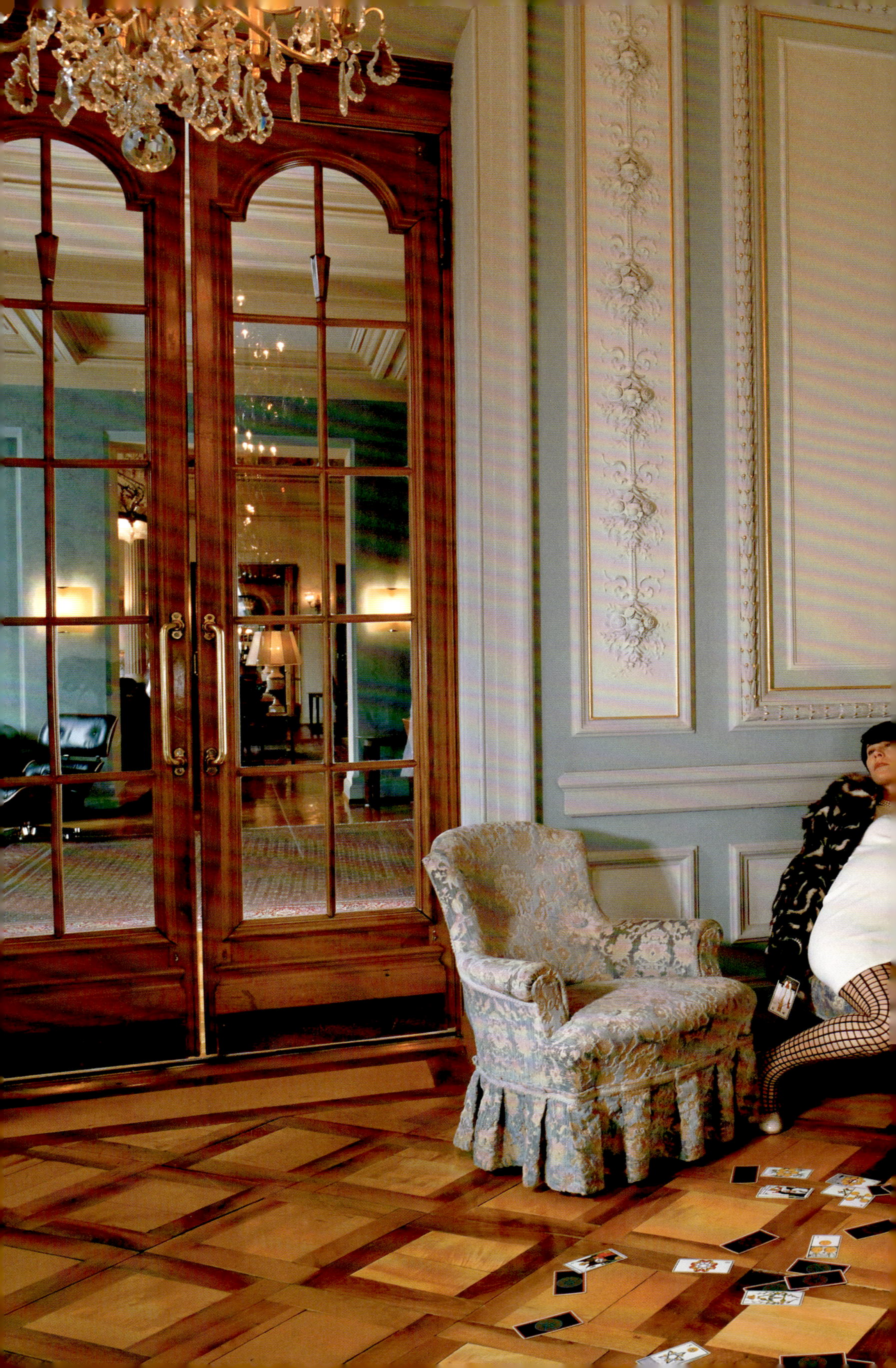

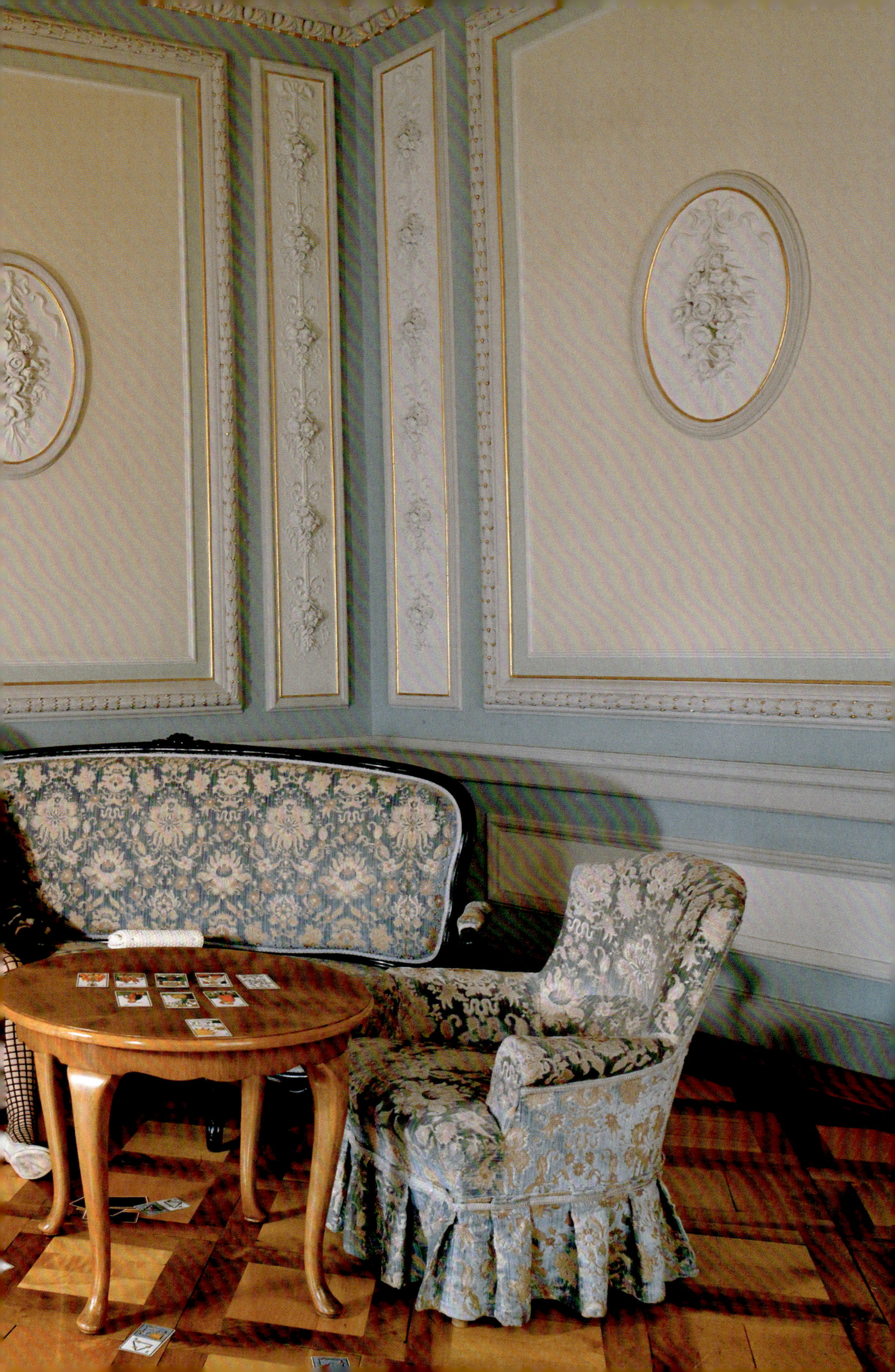

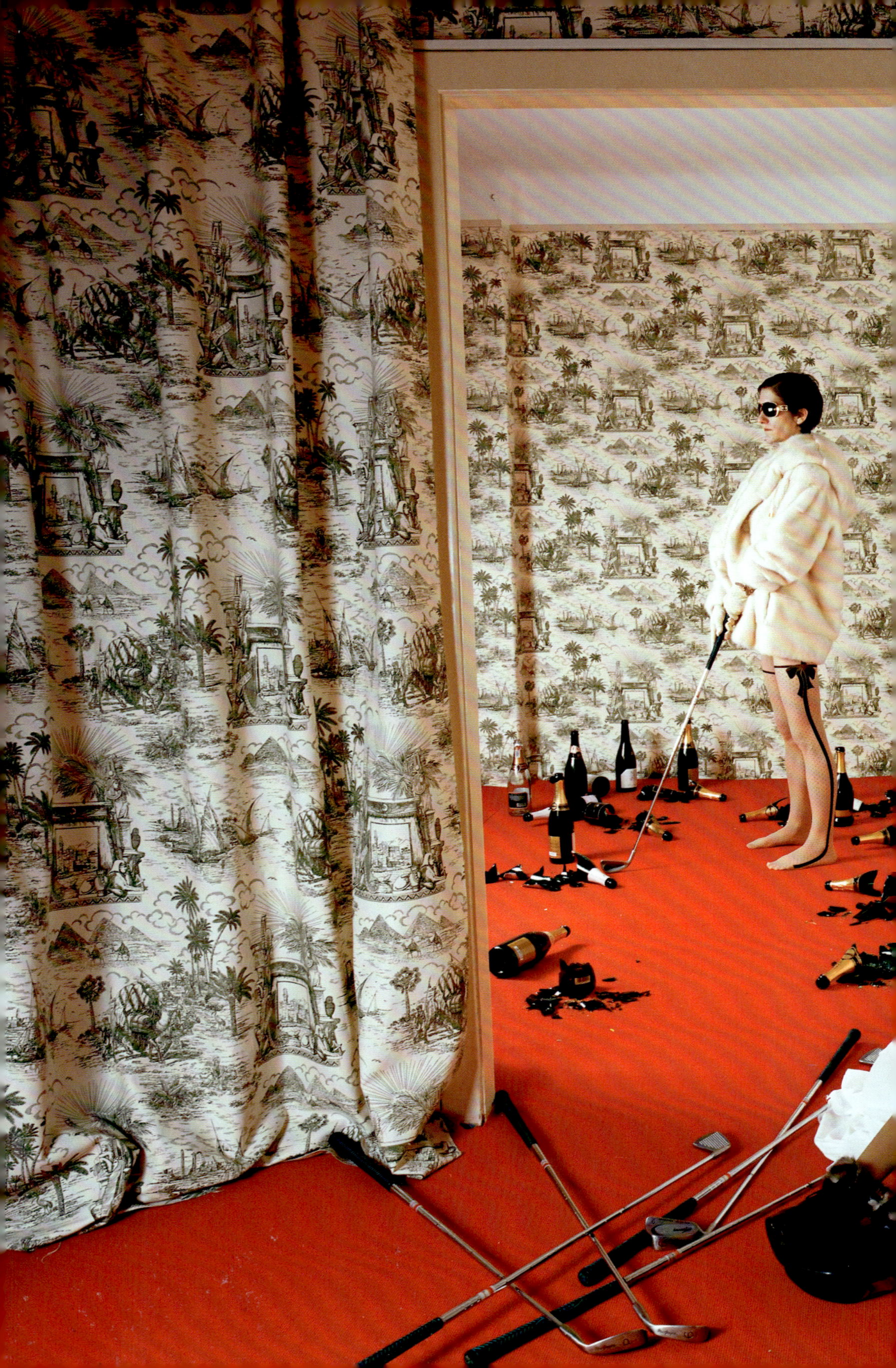

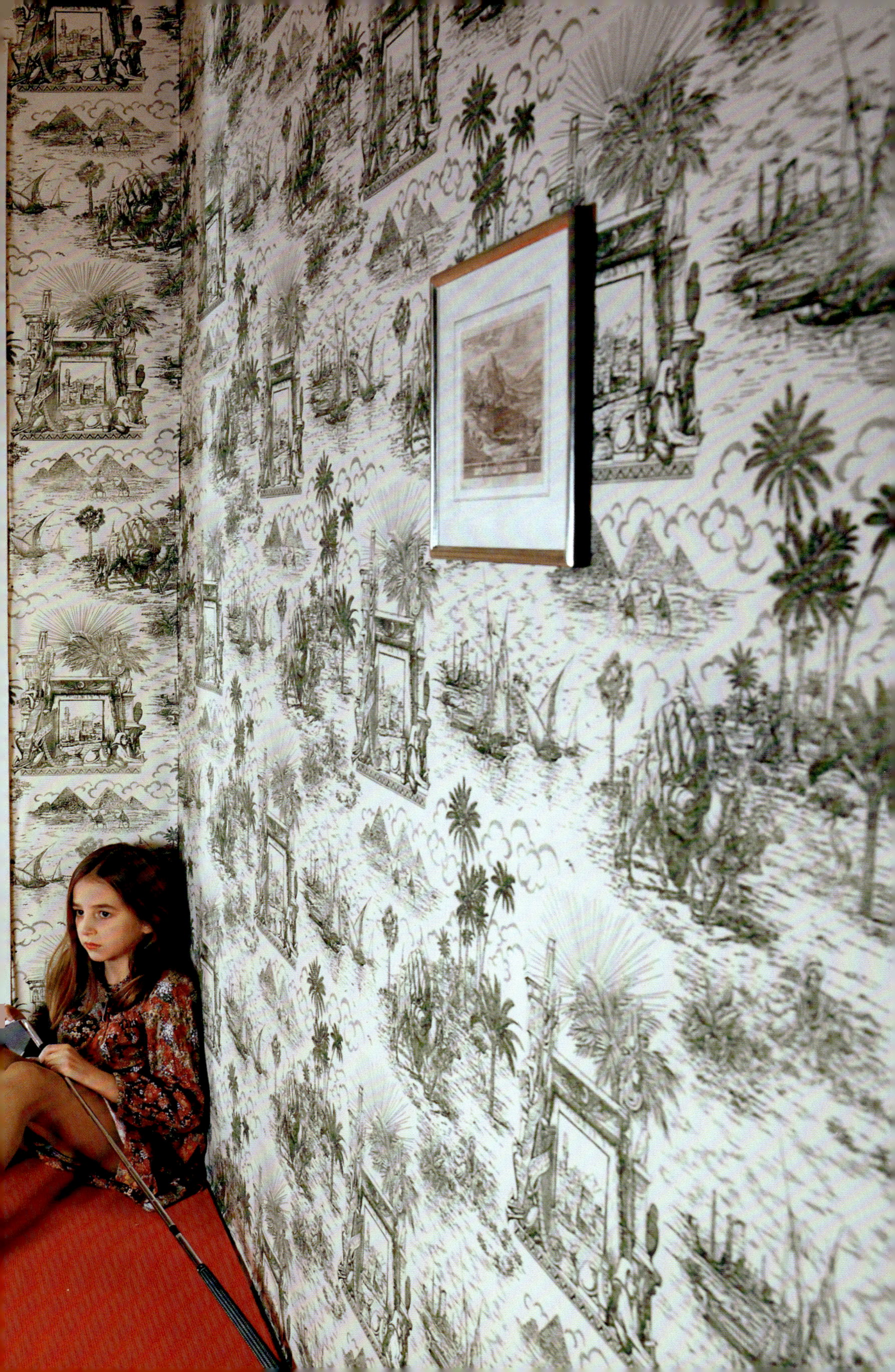

gardens, sensing more than seeing the geography of stalks and leaves around him. The defeated peonies bowed and pushed their fragrant heads into the fingers of the grass, while the poppies swayed in the vacuum suck of the coming storm air, cups wine dark in the waning light from the house. The back border of iris stood sentinel in a patch of teeming mint and coriander, whose wet and broken leaves lent an underlying spice to the sweet heavy odor of damp flowers. Once a few steps away from the house, there was no way to know where the growth ended or where it began. He moved through the lowering blue darkness with the help of a reawakened animal sense of immersion in vegetable space, responding to the oxygen exhalation of the thick ferns and crush of flowers as if to puffs of wind on the tight, exposed expanses of skin. He passed under an arbor choked with spent wisteria, furled morning glories and pearly clematis; petals of curled dog roses lay strewn on the grass and flagstones glowed like flicks of sea foam; the mysterious coil of snails clung like sea urchins on the painted wood. With each step his feet sank in the verdant moss and leaves of grass, minute twigs giving way under the soles of his feet, dandelion fronds lapping at his ankles. From the dark thickets of the forest's edge, a throbbing pulse of wild honeysuckle pushed in waves through the damp air.

Down, down the slope towards the old orchard, the grass now reaching thigh deep, whispering and rippling as small rain does on the surface of a lake, the back of the overlapping fronds arching blue-white in the growing moonlight. Brushing against his bare legs, it was like sinking into a pool of phosphorescent weeds, or a lagoon of rare Mediterranean aquatic phosphorescence, a dream once had about diving into electric water, sparkling hanging swaths of algae, breath held looking back up through the ocean's surface to the distorted stars in the sky above. A weightless pressure enfolded his body, guided him with a current to the stand of trees on the lowering slope, a reef of cropped apple trees clustered with hard green fruit that would become small obscure apples, sour-sweet and pungent—lady apples, damson kings and rose blush. He reached up and let his palm float against the low-hanging branches, something electric between skin and skin.

He repeated to himself the words they had spoken last night, saw again that face through the voice on the telephone line, an image that only memory could invent, features molded in the mind's eye by the push and pull of time, love, and familiar contempt.

The last phrase hovered on his lips—

With sudden violence the wind swelled in a powerful current from behind him, beating down the grass and whipping fallen leaves against his legs, twisting so that the grass parted like an arrow towards the greenhouse. As he turned, he both saw and felt the faint, magnetic penumbra that surrounded the greenhouse as a halo of green light, glowing steadily through the thick humidity with the lure of a beacon. He was pushed towards it, led down the undulating path formed by the wind, in a matter of steps buffeted up against the shoal of small glass panes. He pressed his face and hands against the slick surface and saw the source of the light, an old lantern, sitting on one of the righted potting tables.

There was a stillness inside.

The enamel surface of the table had been recently cleaned, and it gleamed like an operating table in a surgical amphitheater. On its surface was an arrangement of gardening tools placed like implements with yet unidentified purposes, mysterious and portentous and grave, casting unnaturally sharp and distended dark blue shadows on the white surface. As he shifted his gaze from one implement to the next and back again, the rippled glass of the greenhouse walls rhythmically distorted and distended the image of each object, creating the peculiar impression that the limbed metal was somehow breathing, patiently waiting to be taken in hand again. The greenhouse, and everything in it, seemed to throb with light, pulsing like a heart under glass.

His hands twitched on the damp surface, groping—

Something sudden made him turn towards the forest, a sound or a movement, a change in the current of air, he couldn't be sure. Above the blue-black silhouette of the trees he saw the red pulse of intra-cloud lightning. Those last words rose again to his lips, the voice conjuring the face.

*

Little Sister woke to the whisk-like beating of Maurice's wings against his cage.

"No dice!" he squawked, "No dice! No dice!"

She watched his silhouette flutter excitedly to and fro on his twig perch against the blue-black night and shivered in the summer heat. She didn't like to be left alone, especially on a night like tonight, with a storm coming. There was no use in tucking into bed, not in this heat, where there was no

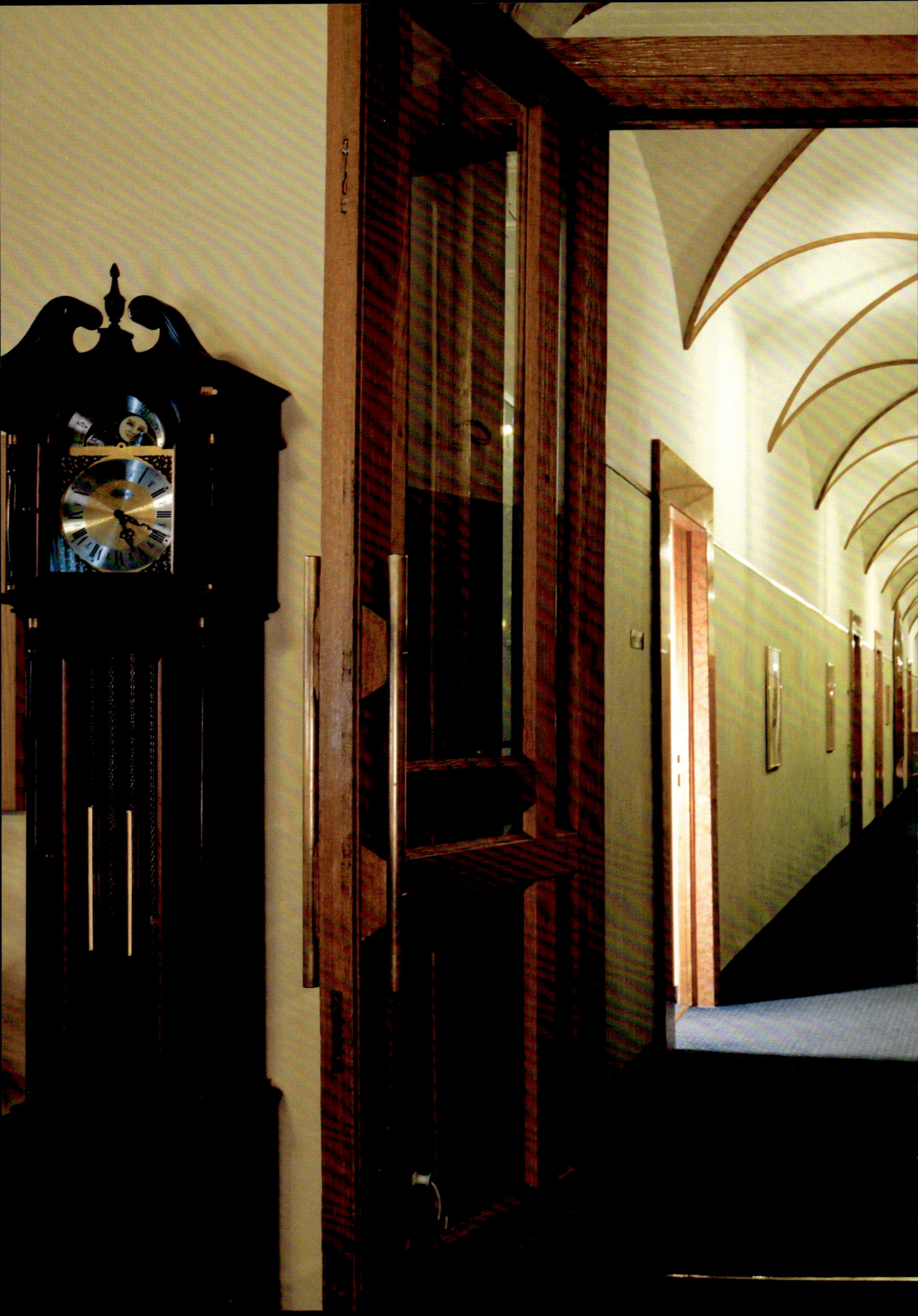

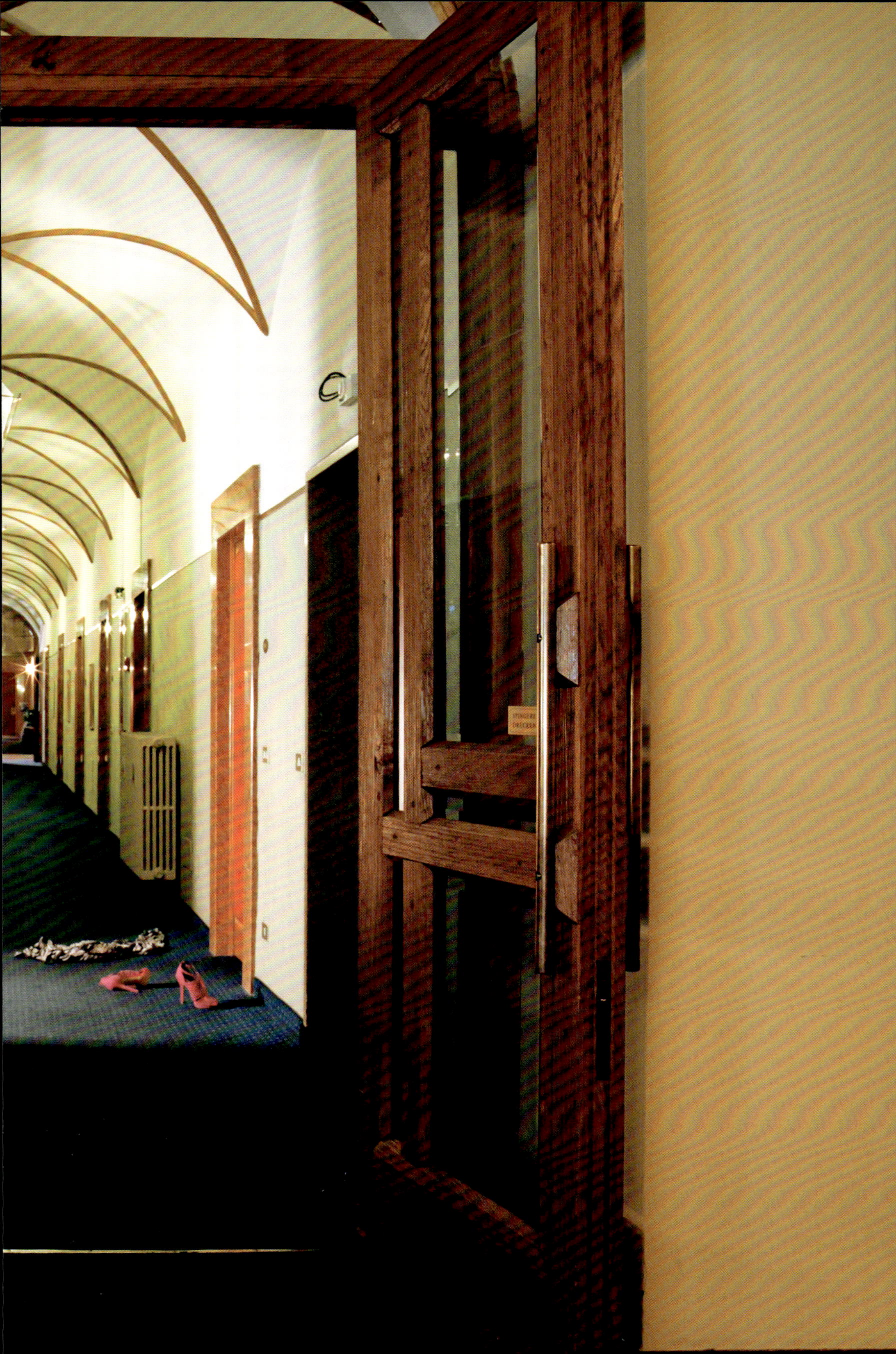
SPINGERE
DRÜCKEN

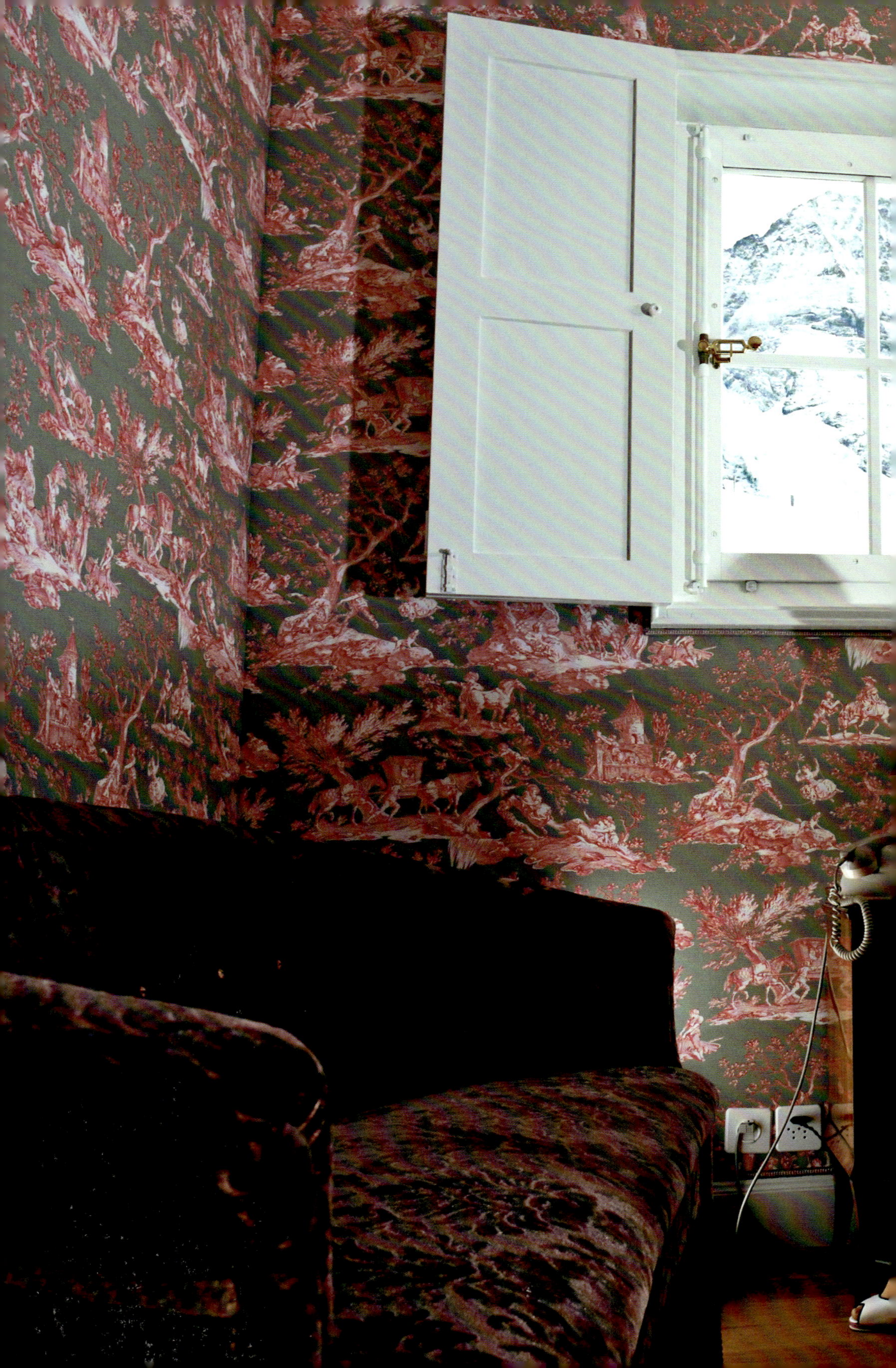

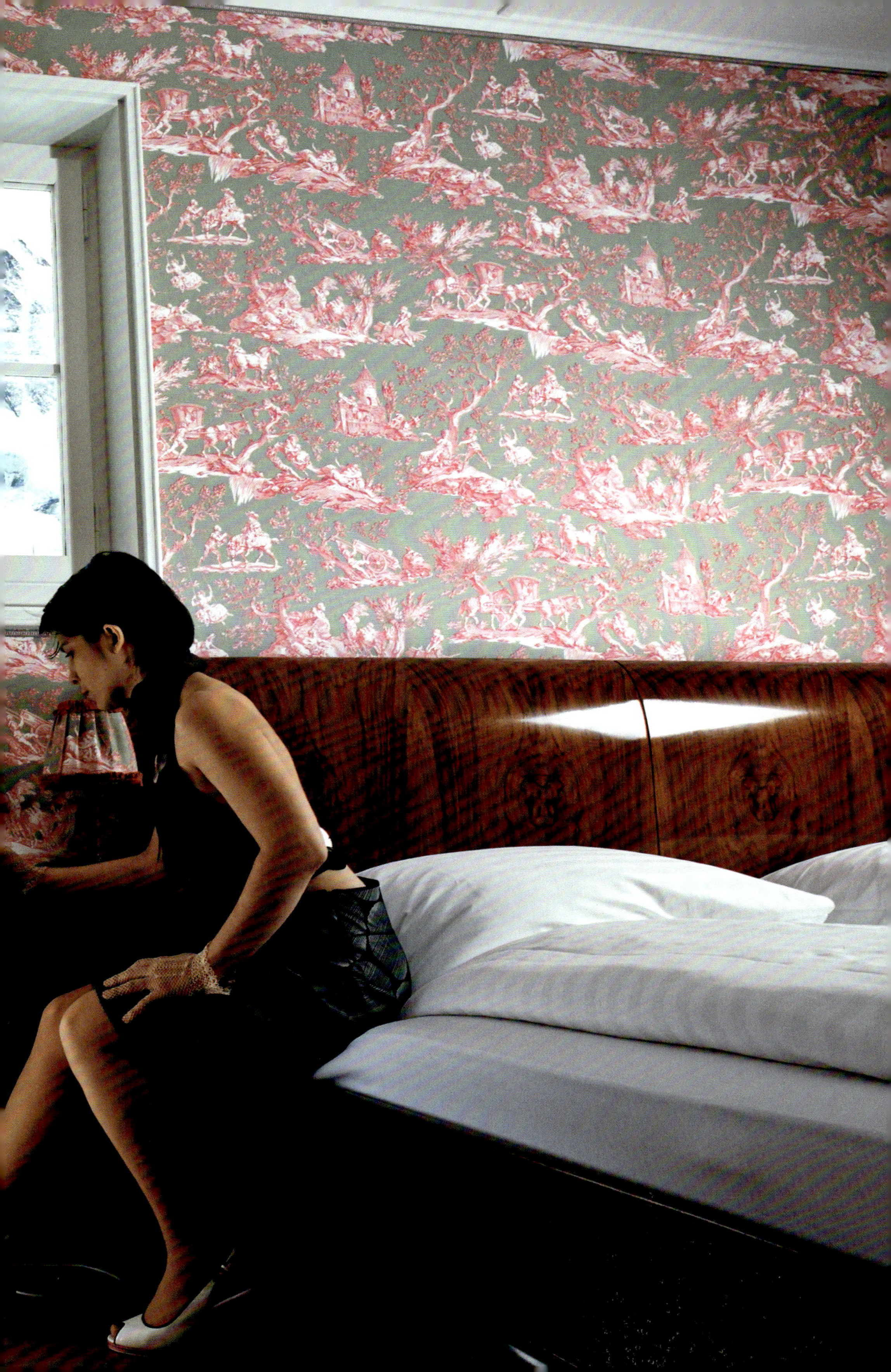

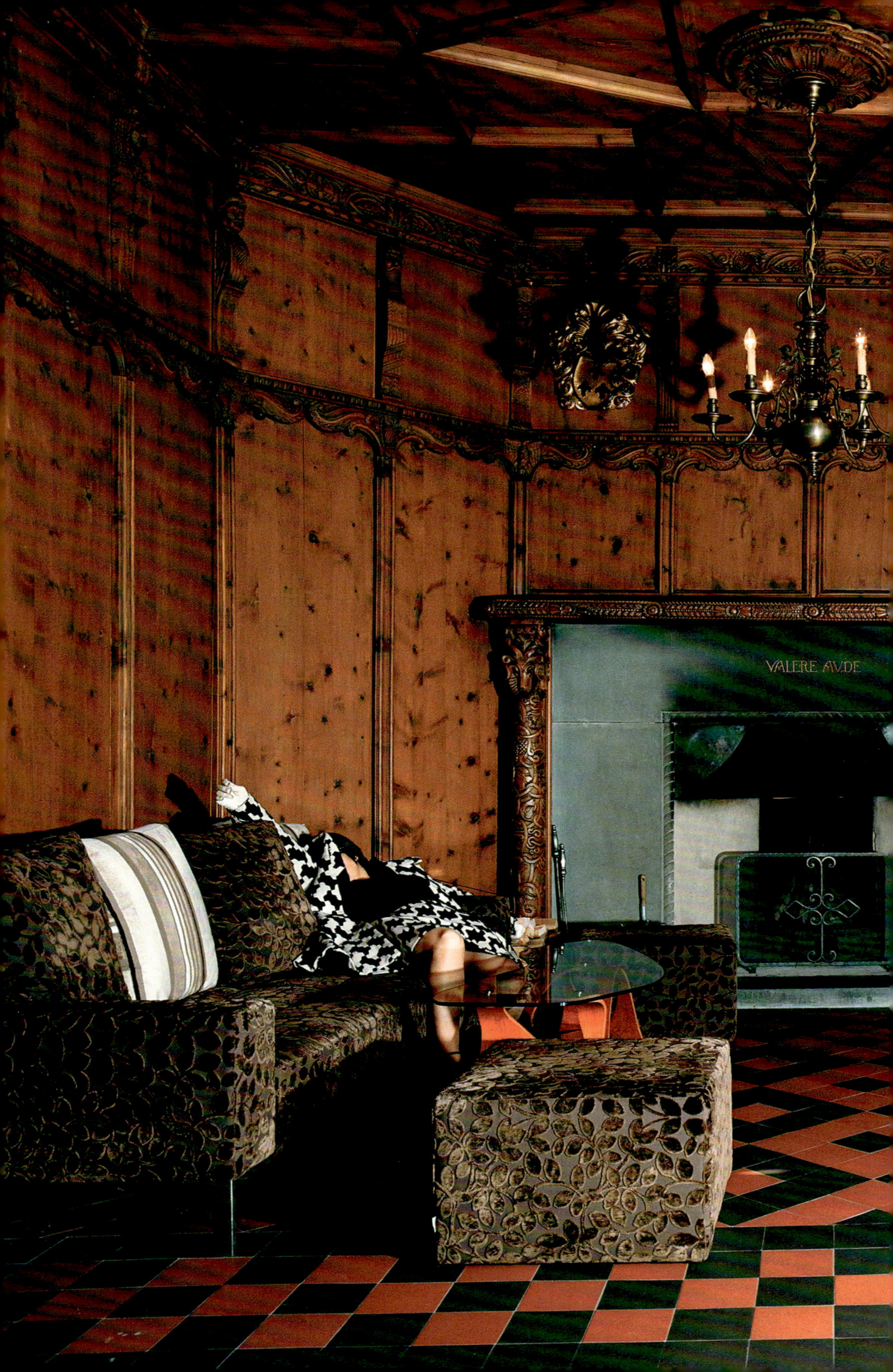
VALERE AVDE

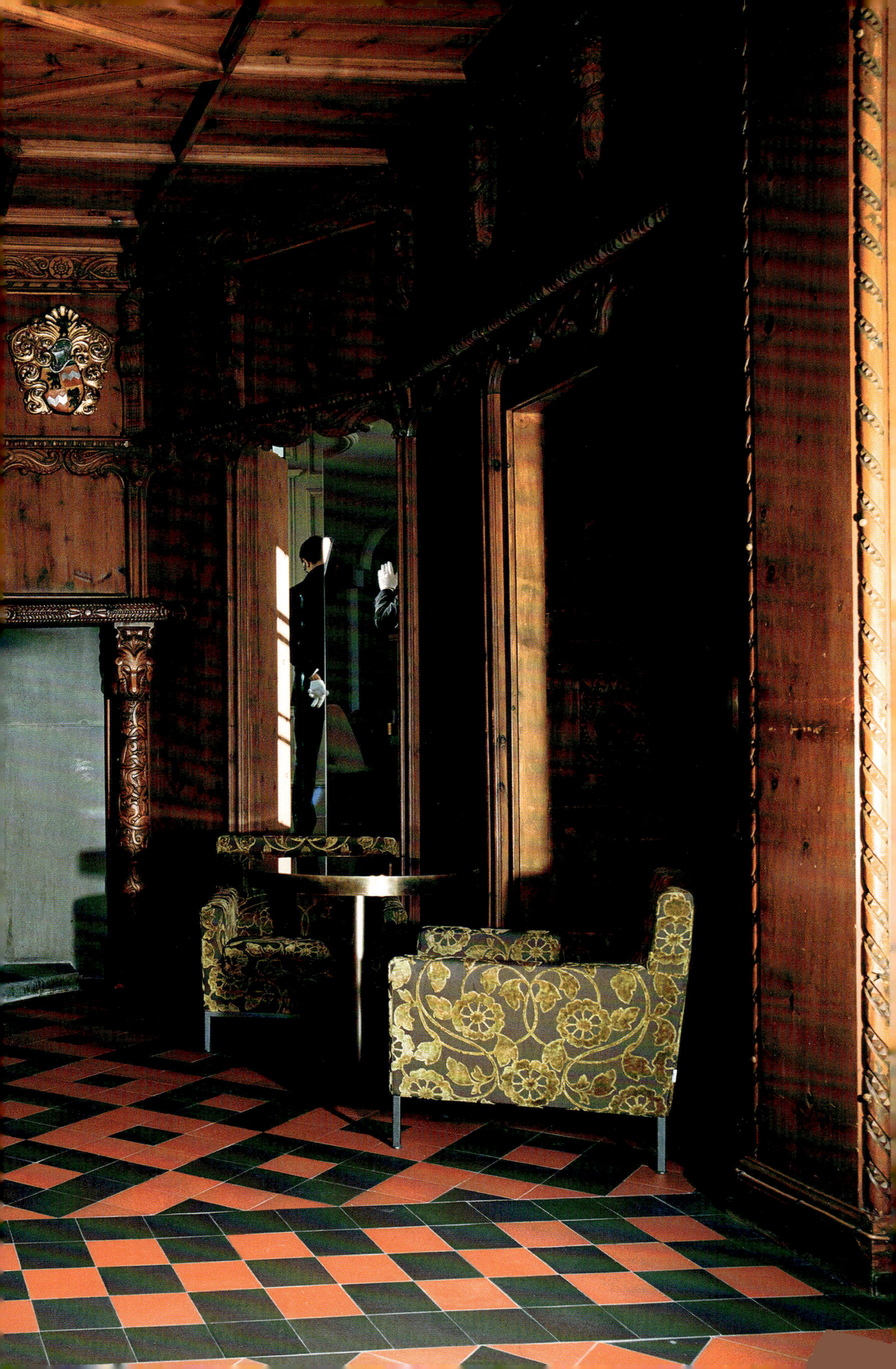

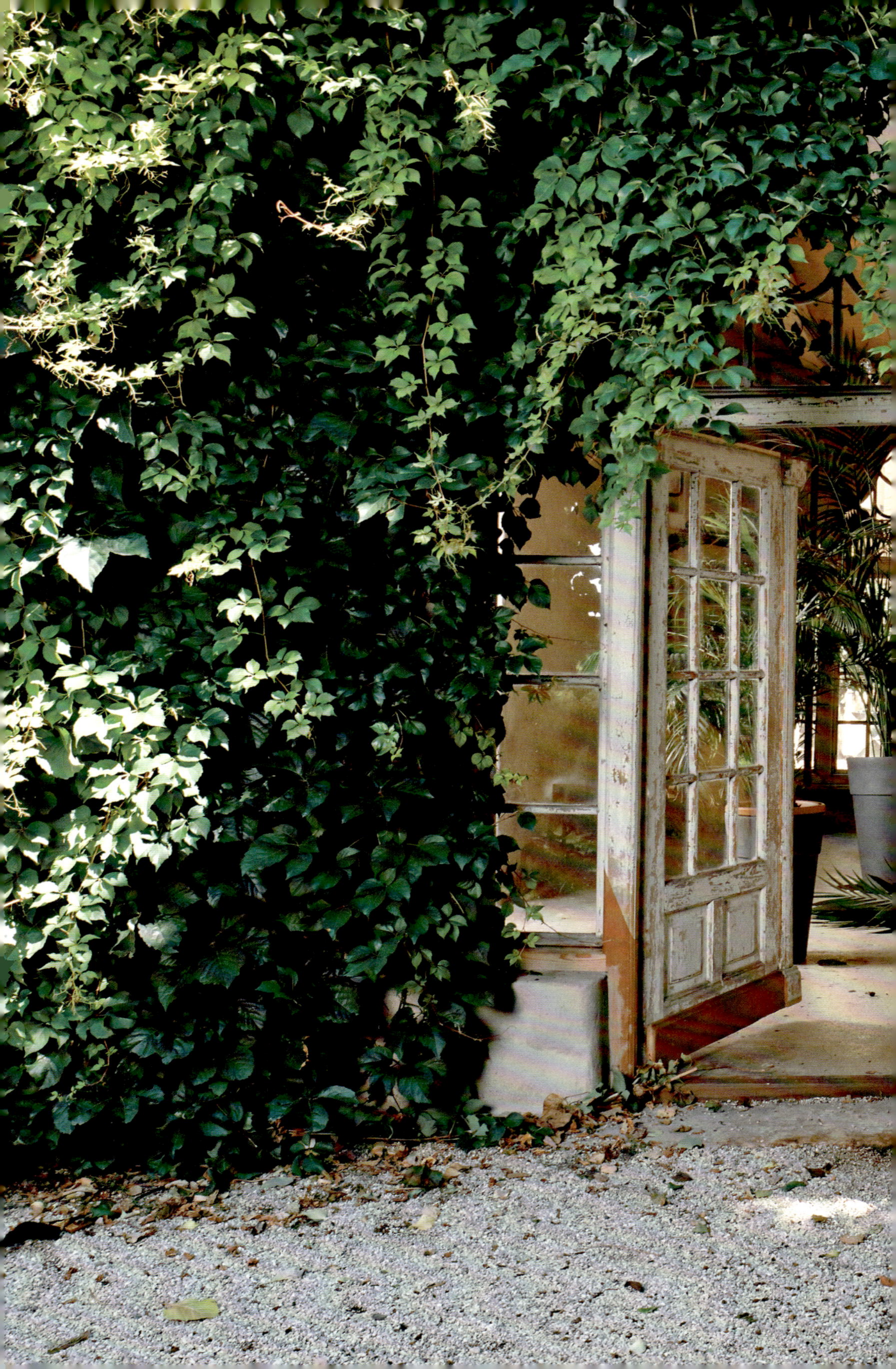

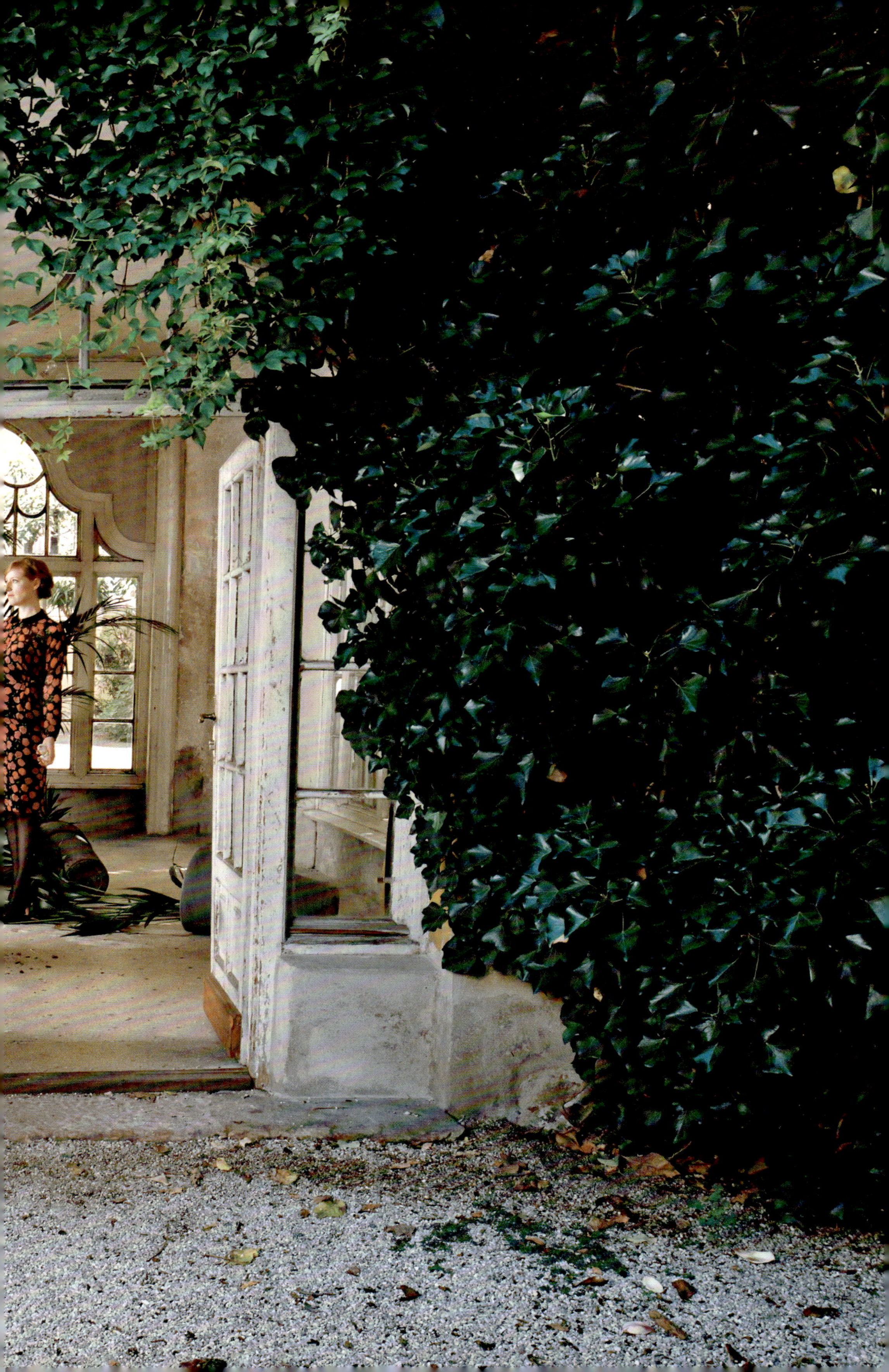

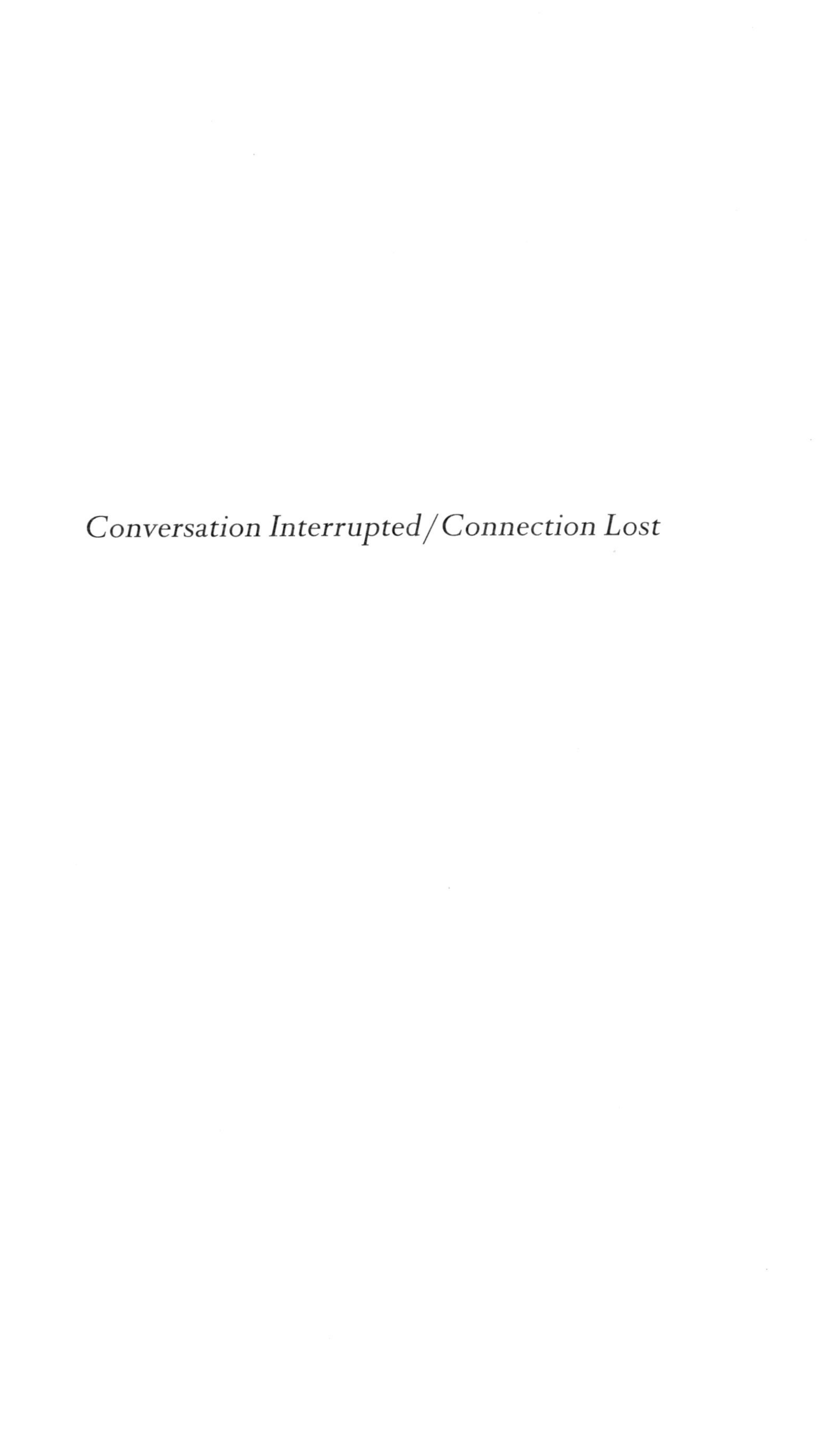

Conversation Interrupted/Connection Lost

LADY SPEAK LOW

1   pony jigger gin
1   pony jigger sweet vermouth
½   jigger crème de violette
½   jigger crème de roses
½   jigger fresh cream
1   dash orange bitters

Shake with ice, strain and serve.
Garnish with orange peel and
candied violets.

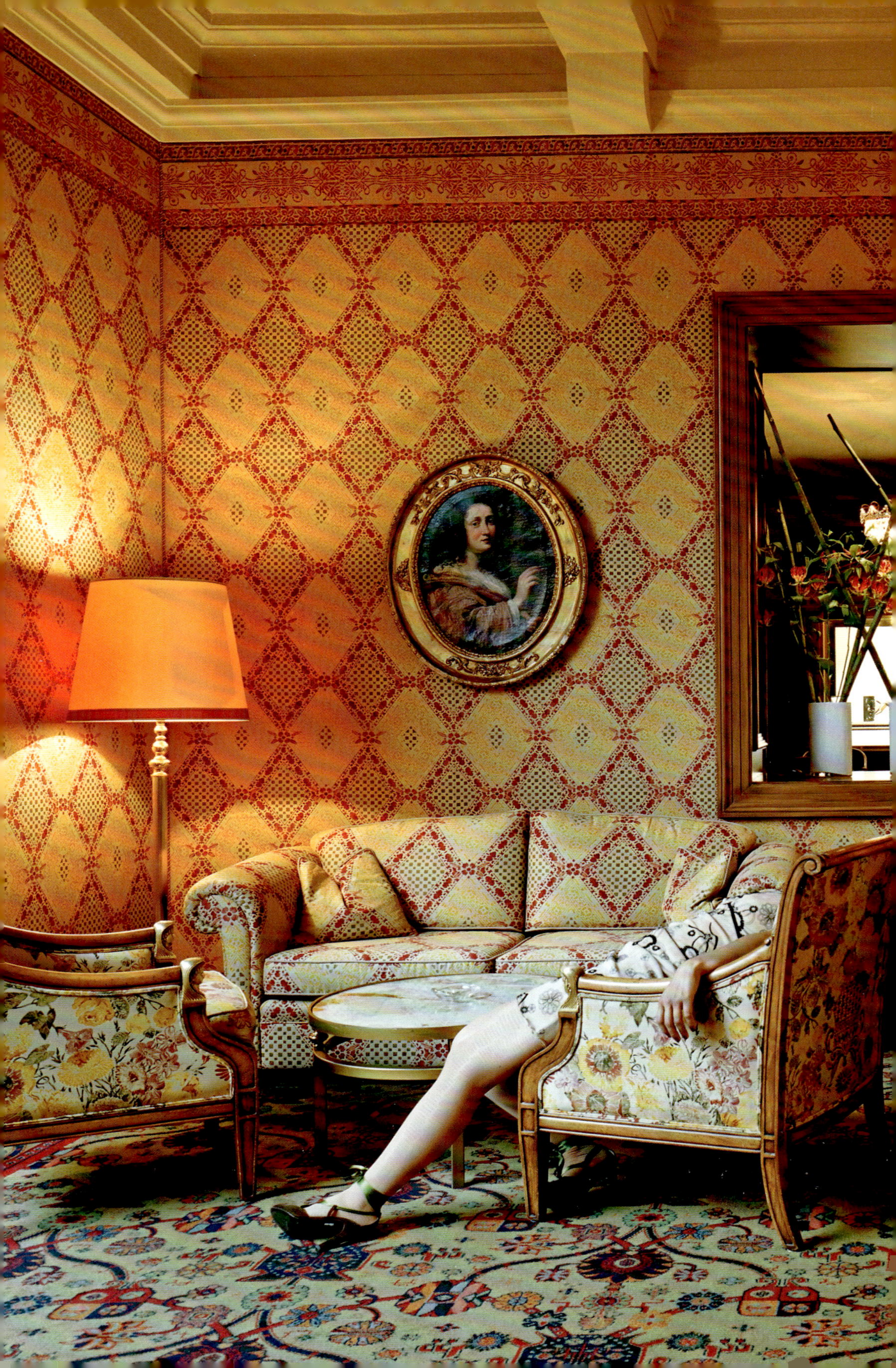

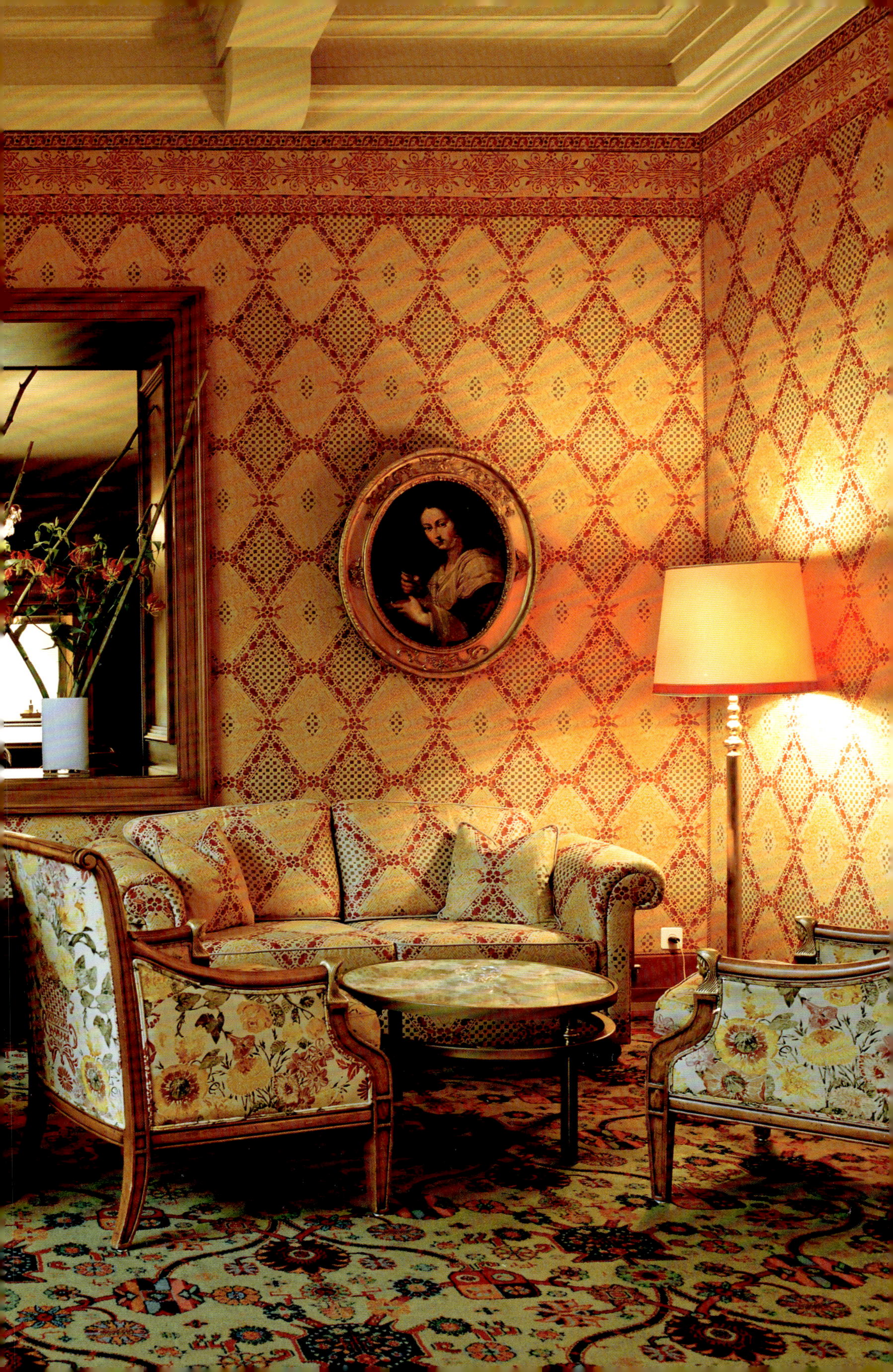

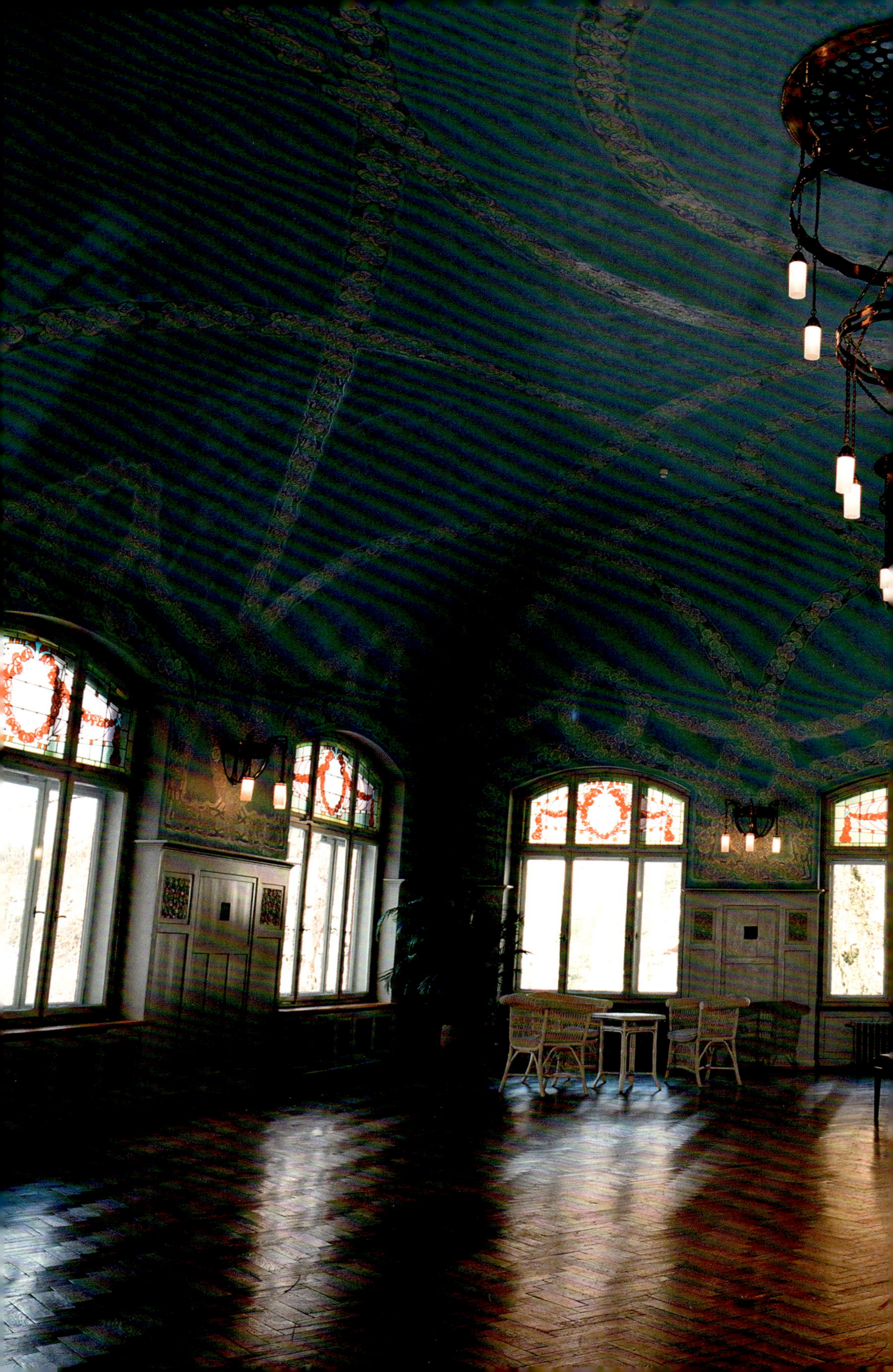

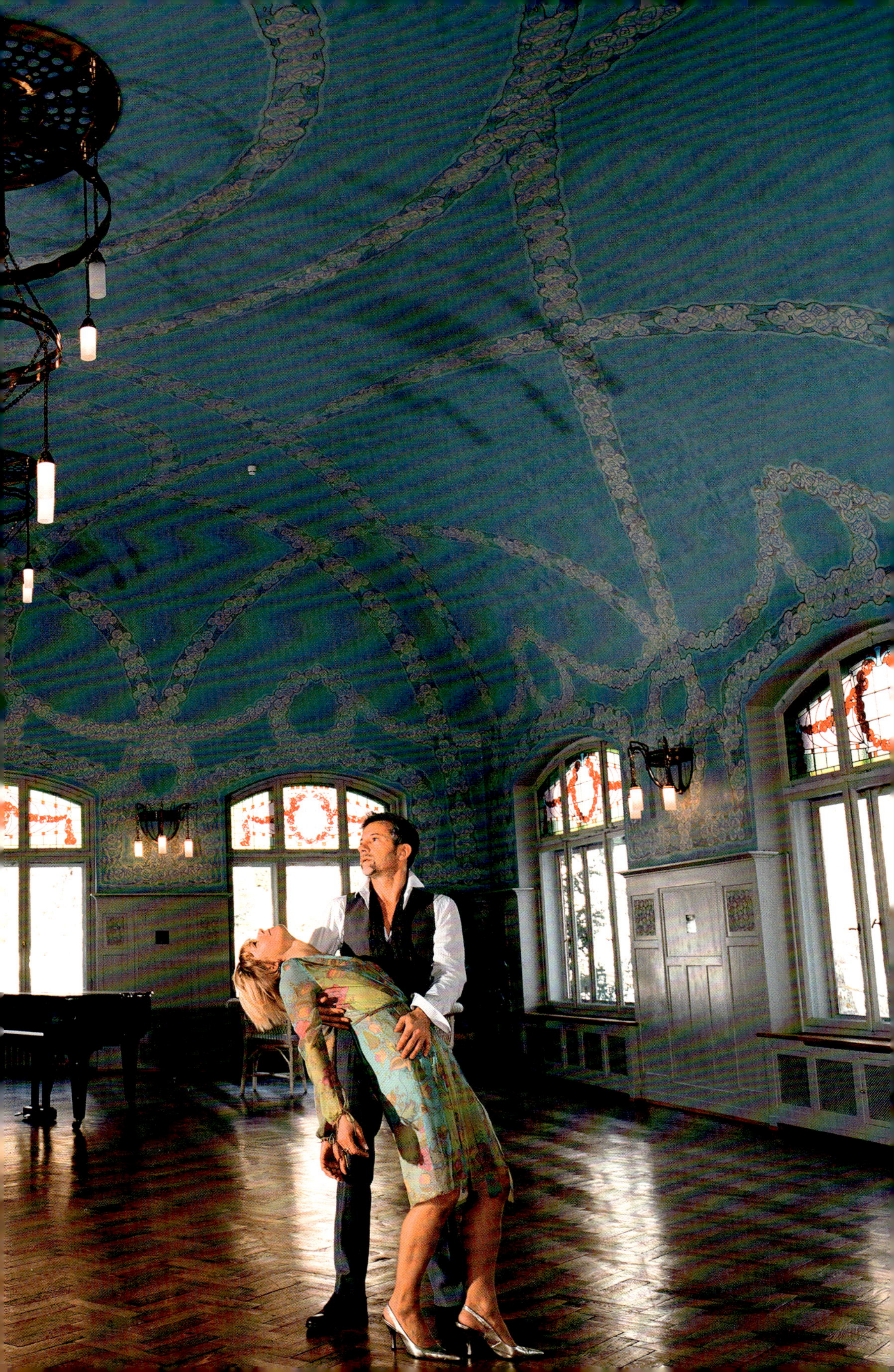

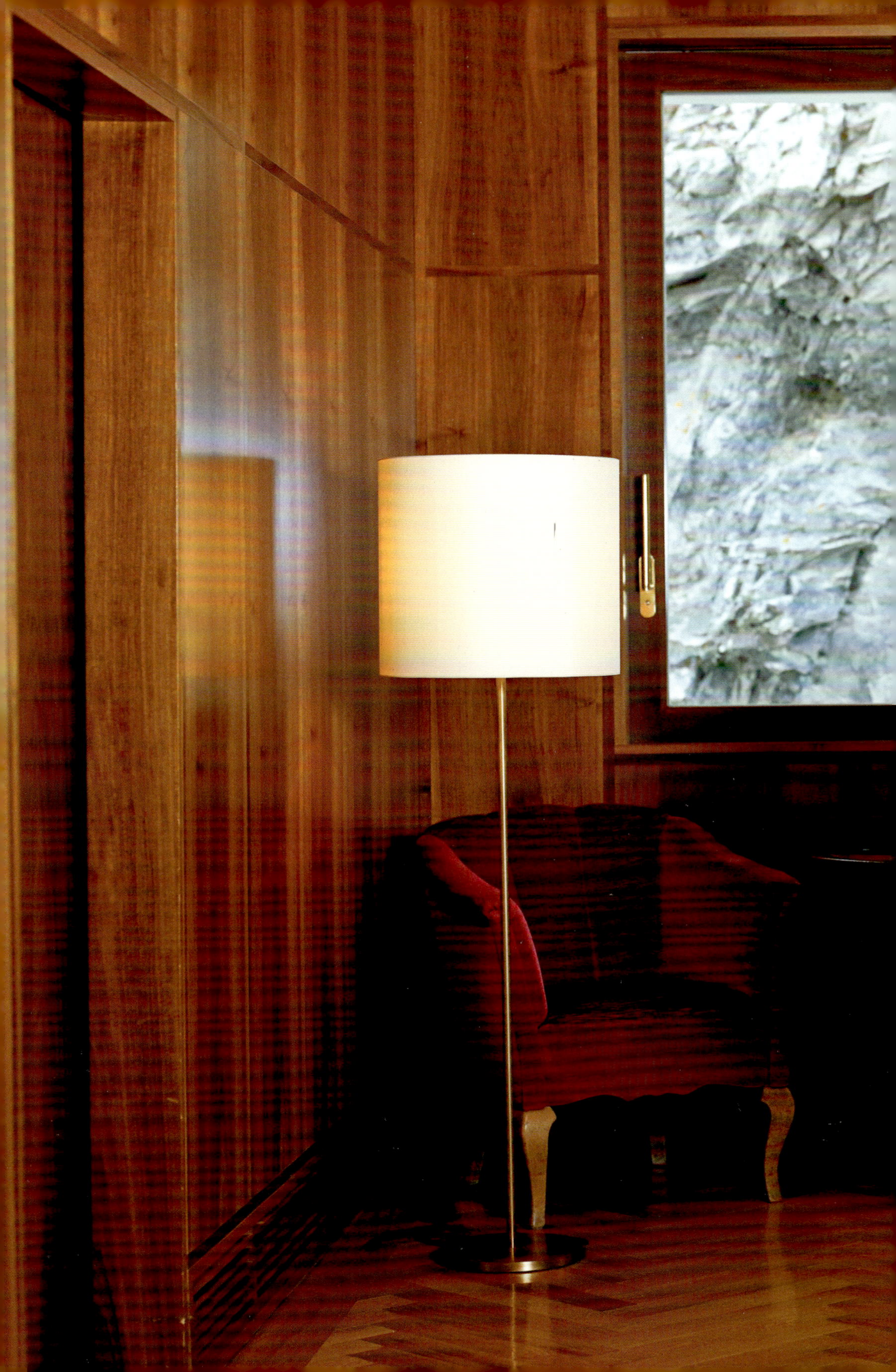

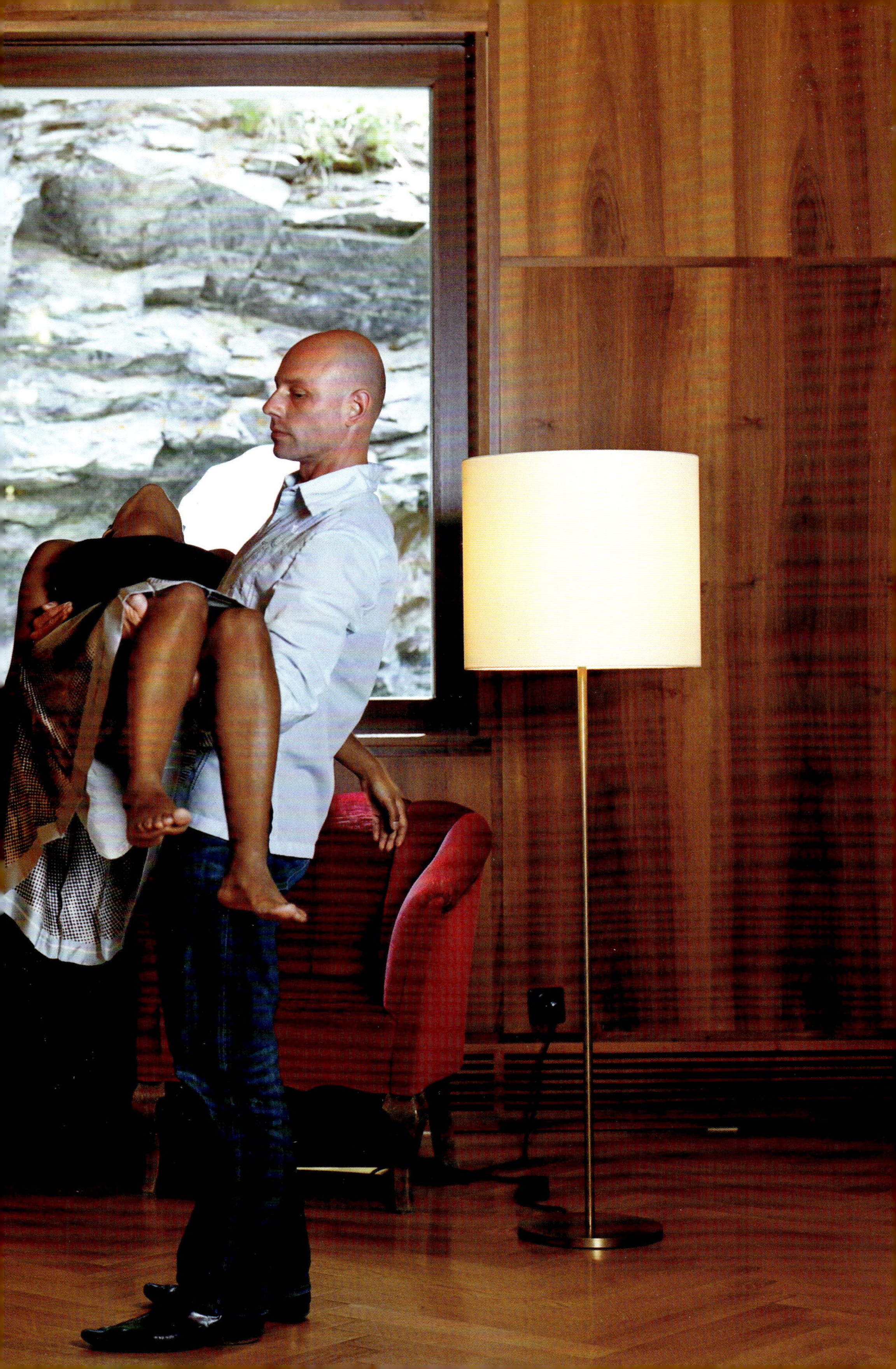

LATOUR, MIRABELLE (1891?–1932?) born Mary Pratt. Silent-movie actress and burlesque performer. Little is known of her early life; first solid documentation is of several tours of the Empire wheel (theaters in the western US) with the George Moody Burlesque Company, where she was billed as the "girl-singer" under the name Millie Pratt. She is rumored to have left the company in 1914 and eloped with the "top-banana" comedian of the company to Los Angeles, but there is no record of the marriage. Later in life, LaTour insisted that she left for financial reasons. While she continued to perform on stage, LaTour began to receive small roles in the burgeoning Hollywood silent film industry. She is best known for her claim to the title role in *Vice*, Erich von Stroheim's controversial adaptation of the Marquis de Sade's novel *Histoire de Juliette ou les Prospérités du vice*, which was never given public screening and is believed lost. During filming, the high security on the closed set and severe non-disclosure clauses in employee contracts fueled rumors of the film's pornographic content, including unsubstantiated details of a scandalous scene involving the Pope.

The discovery of a cache of original silent-era films in 1978 in a Yukon, Ontario, landfill, still in their original tins, has raised hopes that some of the censored material might be among them. The Library of Congress has yet to comment on the matter.

Mirabelle LaTour disappeared while on a publicity junket in central Europe in 1932.

3. Sept.

Thought I could sleep but I can't. I had that dream again, where I'm on the stairs at Mt. Olive. It's not really the stairs, they are much longer and there are windows–you know how dreams are. I keep looking up for someone but there is no one there, just a shadow–hard to describe, more like an outline, something like a photograph, those Hiroshima shadows on stones, dark on dark, an impression of a body that is reflecting the blackness in the stairwell. When I reach the bottom step I turn back, but the staircase is gone and I'm standing in a field full of horses. All the horses are dappled except for one. One is black. The black horse is you.

All those clouds below look unreal, so many miles above the ground, so many miles away from you.
I wish I could tell you how it's not the distance, not the time, how really it's not that I can't live without you–it's just that I didn't miss anything until I met you. How could I?

Confess.

Dearest Carol,

No.

Give my love to Mother,

L.

spaces borrowed and abused, accustomed only to life's fragments, that discouraged the comfort of familiarity, the warmth implicit between people and the spaces they inhabit, as if the geometry of the place itself acted both as springboard and repellent for the subtle weave of emotion that is the complex result of accumulated human experience and all its emotions.

In the end, it seemed she was engulfed by the place. And though I never went back, I expect the rooms were as empty as oceans without her, as there was little trace of her to be found in the things that went to auction, those few orphans—sad, disowned flotsam. What could be blamed, then, for this slow disappearance? It would be easiest to blame her, but I still can't do it. I blame that place.

A hotel, after all, is no place for the slowness of sorrow.

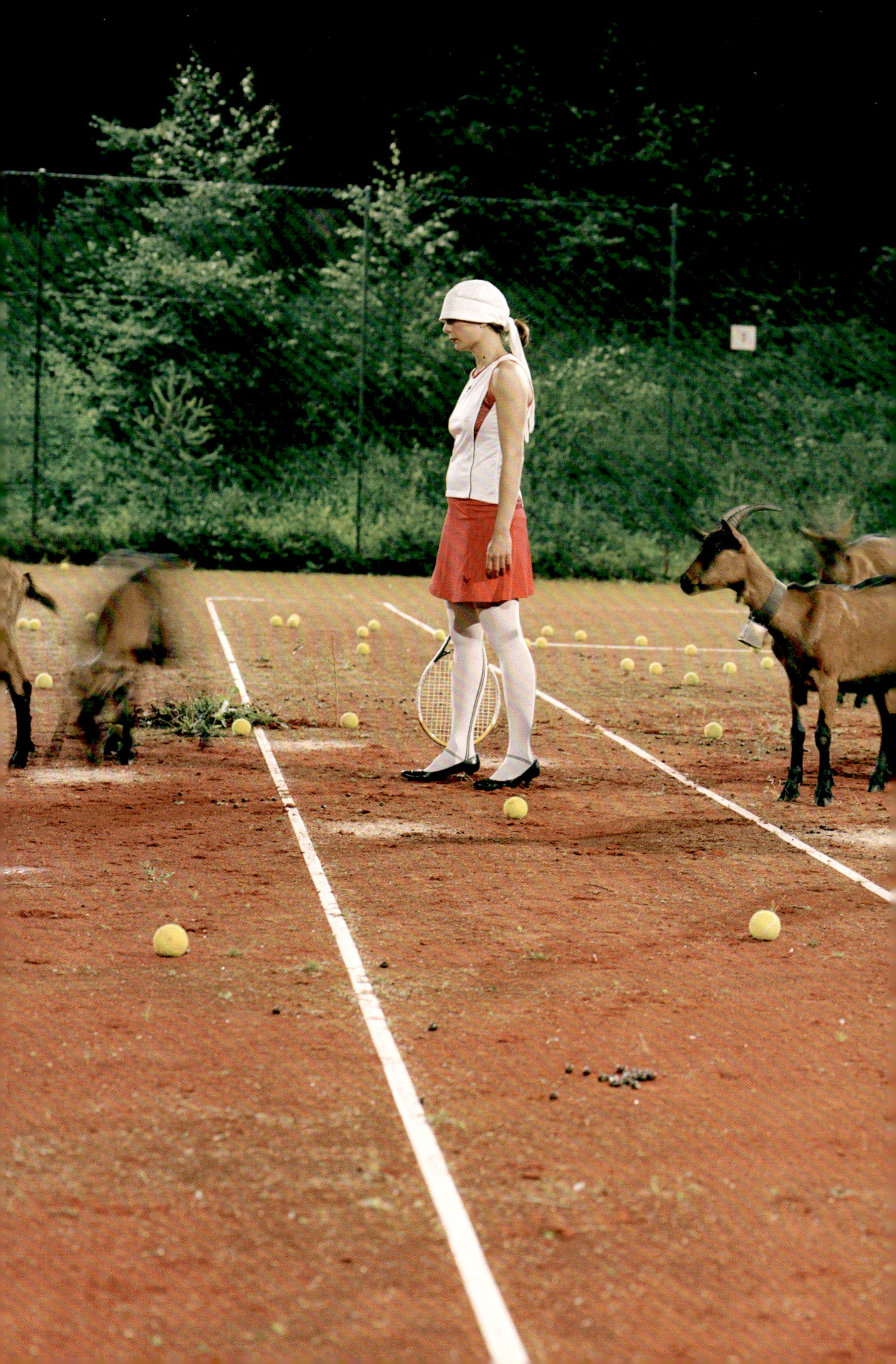

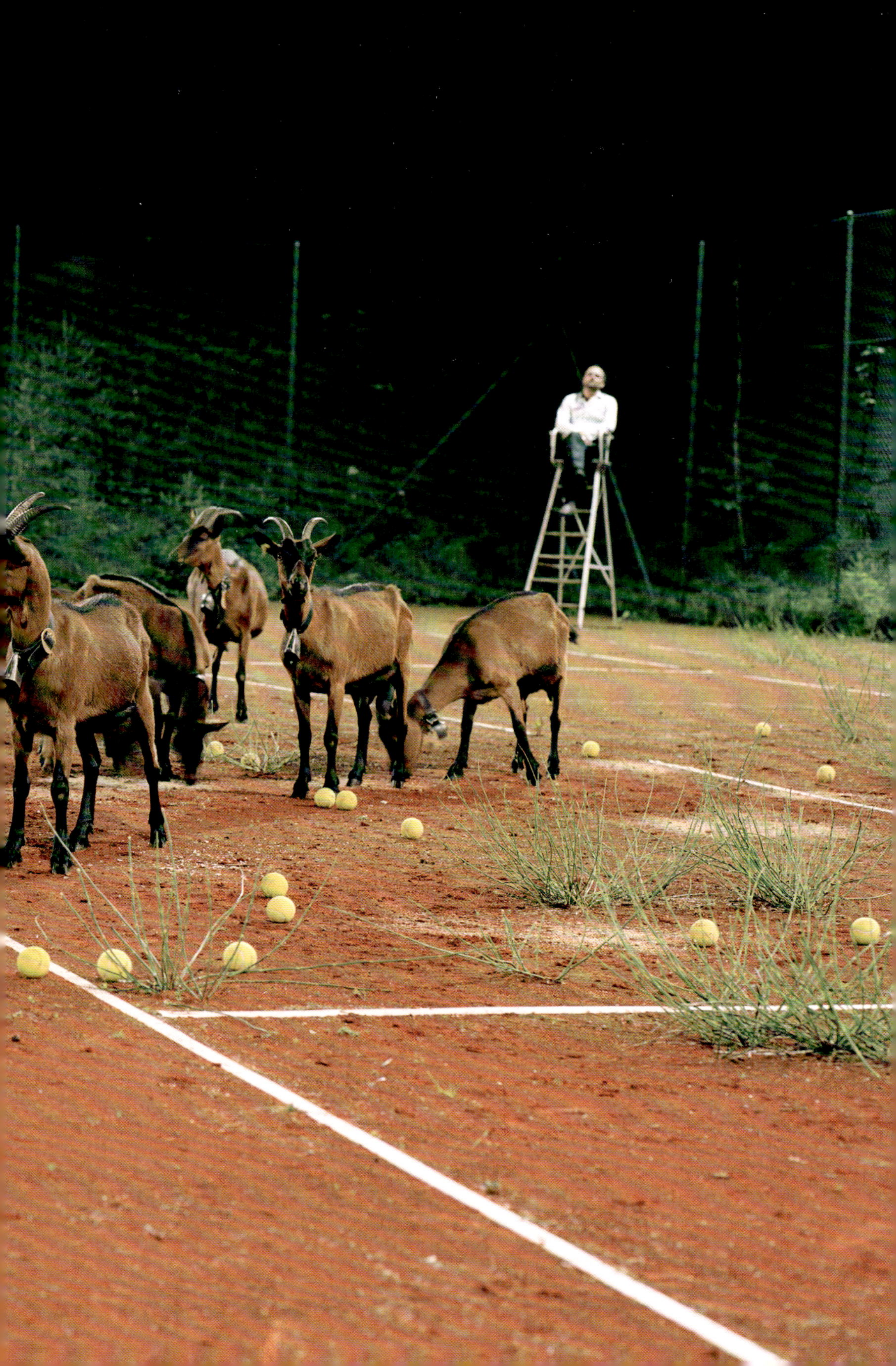

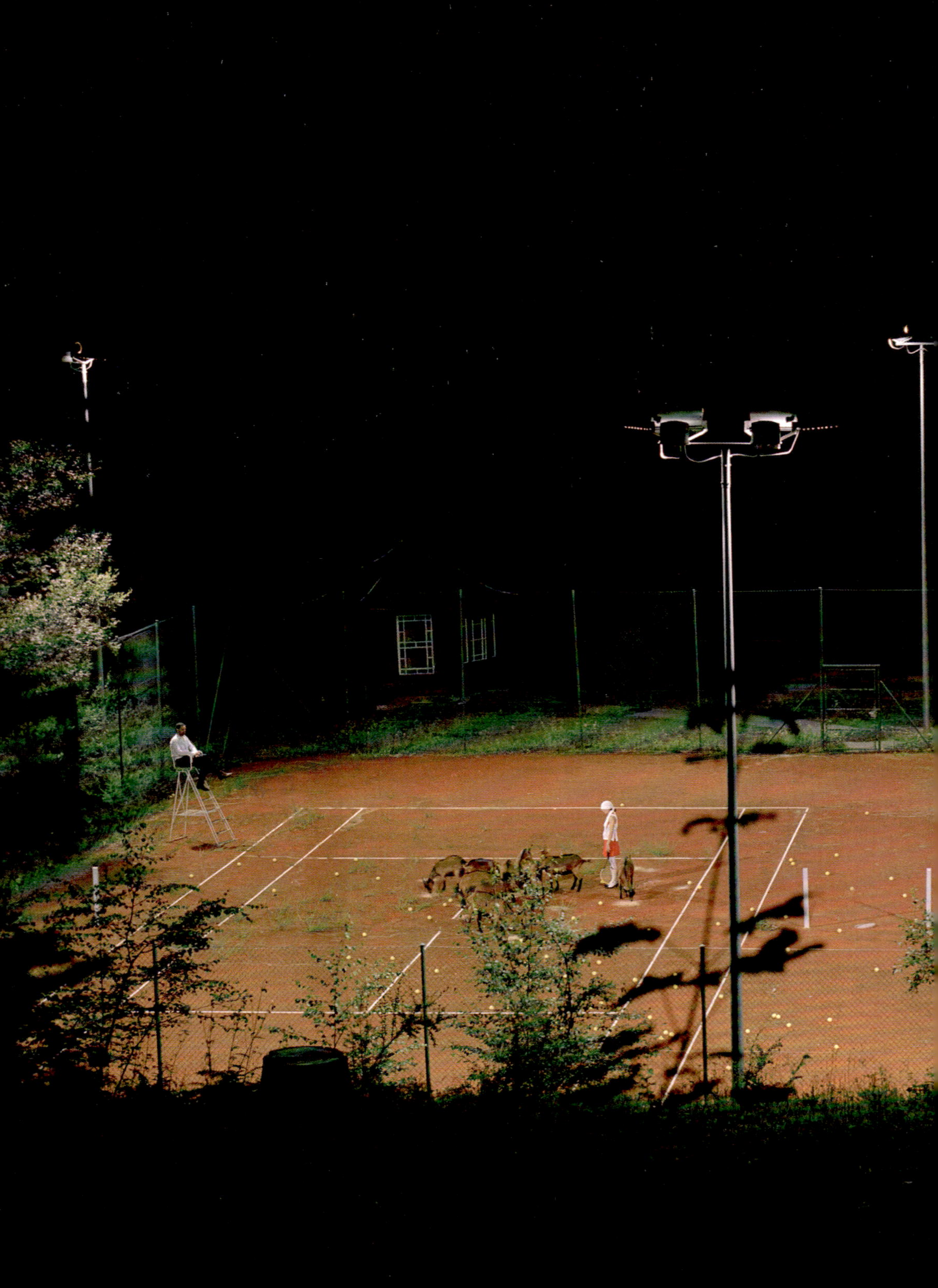

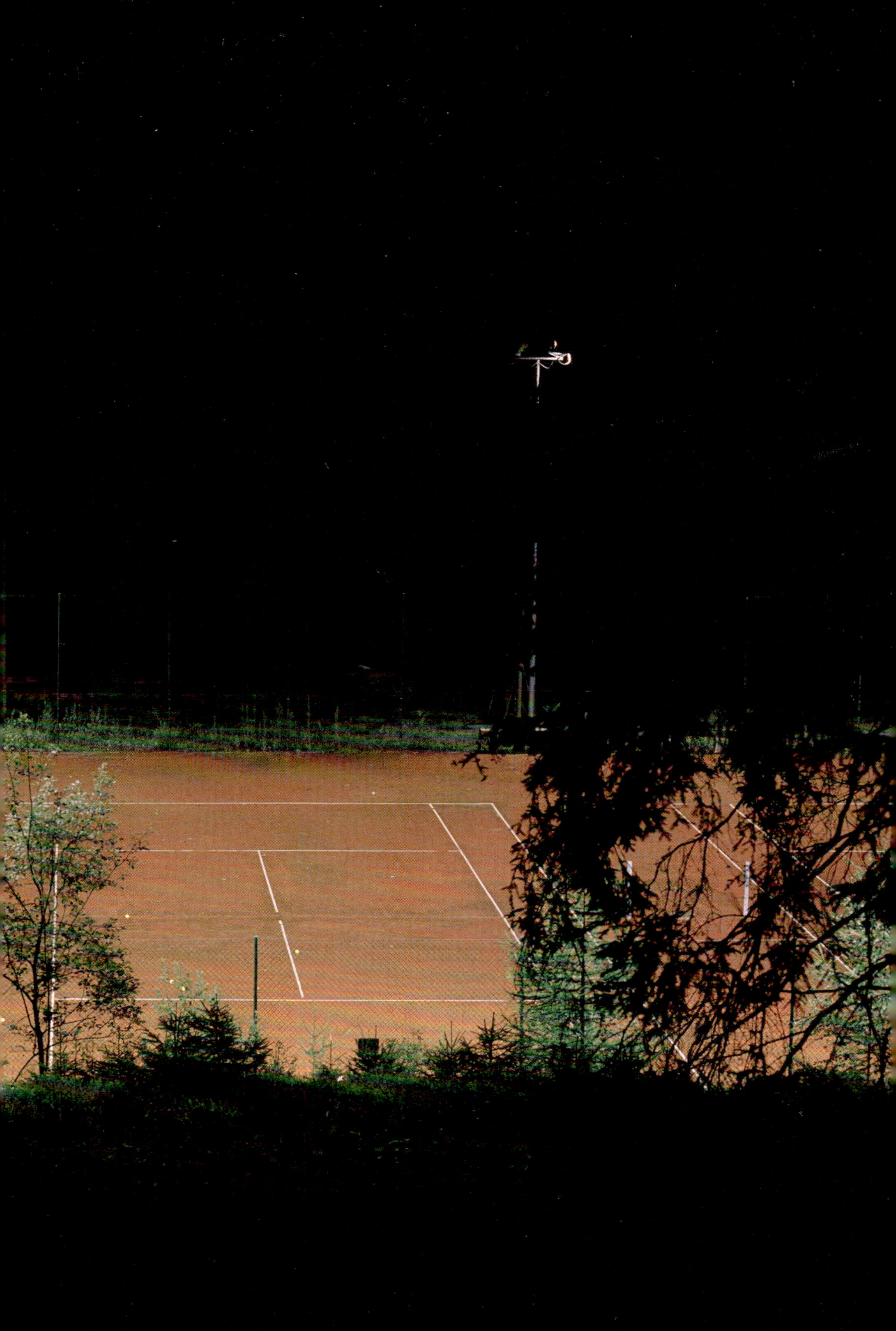

CREDITS

IMAGES (IN SUCCESSIVE ORDER)
01   *wrong shepard, 2010*
02   *missed it!, 2010*
03   *family room, 2010*
04   *leftover, 2007*
05   *sweet dreams, 2010*
06   *i should have had some of that sparkling wine, 2010*
07   *misestimation, 2010*
08   *secret society, 2010*
09   *horse & girl, 2009*
10   *too bright to go out again, 2010*
11   *the snow has no voice, 2011*
12   *it is not a beauty contest, 2007*
13   *why is it so quiet, what are they hiding, 2010*
14   *it is what you fear, 2011*
15   *i let her go. i let her go, 2010*
16   *climbing high, 2010*
17   *ice in the air, 2009*
18   *lost in patterns 2, 2010*
19   *a gift, a love gift, 2011*
20   *lost in patterns 1, 2007*
21   *alhambra, 2010*
22   *relaxation, 2007*
23   *overtime 1, 2007*
24   *overtime 2, 2007*

All images: C-prints on Dibond, 110 × 140 cm, except
07, 09, 16, 17: 100 × 120 cm, and 23, 24:: 80 × 100 cm.

VITAE

CORINNE L. RUSCH
is a visual artist focussing on photography. She lives and works in Vienna.

SOLO EXHIBITIONS (SELECTED)
i am scared, but it is wonderful, FO.CU.S, Innsbruck / *Solo 1*, Fotogalerie Wien /
metaphors in nature, Visual Arts Platform, London / *Space Invasion*, Volkskunde-
museum, Wien / *nightmare angels of the highway*, das weisse haus, Wien / *juggling
wolves*, Photowall Kunsthalle Wien / *suitetalk*, Galleria Laurin, Zürich.

GROUP EXHIBITIONS (SELECTED)
Die nächste Generation III, Traklhaus, Salzburg / *Foto-Auktion*, WestLicht, Wien /
fotoszene.gr, Bündner Kunstmuseum, Chur / *Triennale Linz 1.0*, Landesgalerie,
Linz / *real lives, real stories*, project space, Kunsthalle Wien / *ich ist eine andere*,
MOMENTUM, Wien / *Plateau-Raum für 2*, Forum Stadtpark, Graz / *Make believe*,
Bieler Fototage, Biel / *Editionen*, MOMENTUM, Wien / *Curraint d'ajer*, Kultur-
haus NAIRS, Scuol/Tarasp / *8 Positionen*, *INTO POSITION*, Wien / *Bodytalk*,
Fotogalerie Wien / Galleria Laurin, Zürich / Bogn Engadina, Zuoz / MAK Schind-
lerhaus, Los Angeles.

AWARDS AND SCHOLARSHIPS
Förderpreis der Stadt Chur / BM:UKK-Förderpreis für künstlerische Fotografie
Wien / Förderpreis Kanton AI / Förderpreis Graubünden / Atelier Lardelli /
Cité internationale des Arts, Paris / MAK-Schindler Stipendium / Kulturförder-
stipendium Graubünden.

VIRGINIA DELLENBAUGH
is a writer and musician. She lives in Vienna and New York.

COLOPHON

EDITOR: Corinne L. Rusch
TEXTS: Virginia Dellenbaugh
DESIGN: Anna Sophie Bertermann,
Matthias Meyer, Hamburg
COPYEDITING: Kim Green
Translations: Thomas Raab
PROJECT MANAGEMENT KERBER VERLAG:
Martina Kupiak

The Deutsche Nationalbibliothek lists this publication in the Deutsche Nationalbibliografie; detailed bibliographic data are available on the Internet at http://dnb.d-nb.de.

Printed and published by:
Kerber Verlag, Bielefeld
Windelsbleicher Str. 166–170
33659 Bielefeld
Germany
Tel. +49 (0) 5 21/9 50 08-10
Fax +49 (0) 5 21/9 50 08-88
info@kerberverlag.com
www.kerberverlag.com

Kerber, US Distribution
D.A.P., Distributed Art Publishers, Inc.
155 Sixth Avenue, 2nd Floor
New York, NY 10013
Tel. +1 212 6 27 19 99
Fax +1 212 6 27 94 84

KERBER publications are available in selected bookstores and museum shops worldwide (distributed in Europe, Asia, South- and North America).

ISBN 978-3-86678-644-8

Printed in Germany

HEARTFELD THANKS FOR THE SUPPORT DURING THE REALIZATION OF THIS BOOK GO TO: Hotel Bellevue des Alpes / Hotel Castell, Zuoz / Hotel Waldhaus, Sils Maria / Kulm Hotel, St. Moritz / Kurhaus-Bergün / Parkhotel Laurin, Bozen / Hotel Post Hirsch, Spondinig / Grand Hotel Carezza, Karersee / Flughafen Samedan

Johannes Auvinen, Anna Sophie Bertermann, Hollie Bertermann, Heiko Blankenstein, Corina Bless, Barbara D. Brüesch, Johannes Burr, Chimu, Gion Cadruvi, Herta Cadruvi, Eleonora Cenci, Virgina Dellenbaugh, Andrea Fischer, Flo-nostalgische Mode, Andreas Helbling, Robert Holyhead, Paula Hunjet, Petra Hunjet Moison, JOUJA Wiener Pelzwerkstatt, Matthias Meyer, Flora Neuwirth, Natasha Rehberg, Marion Ritzmann, Markus Rössle, Angela Rusch, Carl Rusch, Carolina Rusch-Nigg, Benjamin W. Schelling, Josias Schmid, Oona Schmid, Claudia Spescha, Rebeca Trepp, Flurin Trepp, Chamaine à Wengen

THIS PUBLICATION WAS SUPPORTED BY:
Innerrhoder Kunststiftung, Stiftung Dr. M.O. Winterhalter, Stiftung Erna und Curt Burgauer, Willi Muntwyler – Stiftung St. Moritz

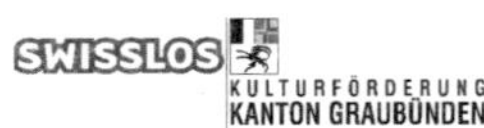